Living
Paganism

An Advanced Guide for the
Solitary Practitioner

By

Shanddaramon

New Page Books
A Division of The Career Press, Inc.
Franklin Lakes, NJ

LIVING PAGANISM
EDITED BY JODI BRANDON
TYPESET BY EILEEN MUNSON
Cover design by Mary Langer
Printed in the U.S.A. by Book-mart Press

To order this title, please call toll-free 1-800-CAREER-1 (NJ and Canada: 201-848-0310) to order using VISA or MasterCard, or for further information on books from Career Press.

The Career Press, Inc., 3 Tice Road, PO Box 687,
Franklin Lakes, NJ 07417
www.careerpress.com
www.newpagebooks.com

Library of Congress Cataloging-in-Publication Data

Shanddaramon, 1959-
    Living paganism : an advanced guide for the solitary practitioner / by Shanddaramon
        p. cm.
    Includes bibliographical references and index.
    ISBN 1-56414-825-4 (pbk.)
        1. Paganism. I. Title.

BL432.S53 2006
229'.94--dc22

2005049141

This work is dedicated
to all those
who are striving
to make Paganism
a viable and serious religion
for the betterment of Gaia
and all her children.

Acknowledgments

I wish to thank my lifelong partner, Mary, and all my friends, students, and colleagues for putting up with me as I have experimented with these practices throughout the years. I would also like to thank all those people who wrote to me about my book *Self-Initiation for the Solitary Witch* to thank me for writing it and to express how it has helped them in their lives. I hope this book will do the same for them and others.

Contents

A Brief Explanation
of the Chapters

Chapter 1: Creating a Pagan Way of Life will discuss in detail the various cycles of the universe and of our lives. We will explore how we can relate to these cycles and how you can develop your personal spirituality through celebrating these cycles. Through these practices you will learn to develop yourself spiritually, to work to improve the lives of others, and to connect yourself to Gaia, the moon, the sun, and Spirit.

Chapter 2: Determining Spiritual Goals will take a closer look at how we can determine our personal spiritual goals and activities to honor the sacred cycles. We will observe those things that we can do for ourselves to make our lives better, more enjoyable, and more spiritual through simple activities and attitudes to life. Activities can be subtle or grand depending on your personal preference. We will also look at practices designed to help others and that celebrate and help us work for the good of Gaia and her children, and we will look at goals and practices that help us develop deep connections to Spirit and our sense of the divine presence in the universe. We will also determine practices for honoring yourself and others as you progress through the many changes and challenges of life. You will learn how to determine your goals through the four elements and the three energies that are part of all cycles. The chapter will focus on helping you develop your own spiritual goals in a complete and balanced way so that you can then learn to apply these goals to the various cycles.

Chapter 3: The Cycles and Their Significance will take a close look at each of the universal cycles—Gaia, moon, sun, and life cycles—and help you determine the significance that each has in your life. Occultists and magicians have long attached significant meanings to different cycles, such as the days or the months. We will observe some of those ideas and, in some cases, I will provide options for finding and developing your own meanings. Once you have determined these things, you can then relate your spiritual goals and their significance to the meanings of the cycles to create a deep and meaningful personal practice.

Chapter 4: Merging Goals and Cycles will help us to learn to apply the goals you identified in Chapter 2 with the meanings of the many cycles of Gaia, the cosmos, and our lives so that they become natural ways to honor the mysteries of life. We will then take what you have determined is significant about each of the cycles from Chapter 3 and combine your goals with these significances so that you can begin to put together a complete program for living a Pagan life.

Once you have determined your goals, you then need ways in which to practice and express them. Pagans celebrate life through rituals. In **Chapter 5: Rituals for Celebrating the Cycles** I will offer suggestions for how you can create your own rituals to celebrate many of the things discussed throughout this book.

Introduction

While I was writing my previous book, *Self-Initiation for the Solitary Witch*, I realized that what I was including in the work for the fifth degree could be no more than an introduction. The fifth degree of my system is designed to recognize one who has dedicated himself or herself to living the Pagan life. To remain true to your spiritual principles in the face of the pitfalls of day-to-day life is quite a challenge. I knew that one day I would have to write more about the topic, and this work is the result. This work is a natural extension to the *Initiation* book, but it can also stand on its own. One can commit to a degree system to learn about Pagan practice and principles and then dedicate a life to living those principles, or one can choose to live a Pagan life without undergoing any degree work. This book is designed as a tool for either goal.

The more I learned, studied, and practiced Paganism, the more I wanted to make it part of my everyday life. It's one thing to learn about Pagan principles and to even develop a personal private practice, but it's quite another to apply those principles to every part of your life. Knowing something is not the same as living it. We can study swimming or playing an instrument without actually doing it, and we can occasionally swim or play some music without actually making those things a central part of our lives. It's the difference between someone who swims once a week at the local pool and someone who devotes his or her life to winning a medal at the Olympics. Spirituality can be much the same. We can go to a ritual eight times a year and maybe take a class once a week, or we can decide that, in addition to the rituals and the classes, all the other parts of our lives should also reflect those things we are learning and practicing. In other words, we must decide if we are going to just talk the talk or if we are going to walk the walk. I decided I wanted to do the latter.

But, how do you do that? How do you truly live the Pagan life? First, you must be clear about your Pagan principles. Some may say that living the Pagan life means just doing whatever you want to do. I argue that Paganism is not hedonism. If we are going to believe that Spirit exists within and beyond all things, then we are responsible for how we act and respond to each other. If all things are sacred, then all our interactions are equally as sacred. Learning to act this way requires a certain daily act of courageous commitment. It requires occasionally doing what is right for the whole rather than for the satisfaction of the self. This focus on the totality of experience is truly spiritual.

What I discovered is that the way to live a Pagan life is to celebrate and honor the many cycles of life and the world in which we live. Our whole universe is composed of cycles, but we have gone out of our way as a society and culture to ignore those cycles. Yet we wonder why we feel disconnected. We base our lives on the clock and the calendar—both of which ignore natural cycles. We rise with the alarm clock rather than the sun. Few people are conscious of the changing phases of the moon, or that the word *month* itself was derived from the word *moon*. This is because the beginning of the month was once determined by the priests of a community and was based on the first appearance of the new moon. Now, however, the moon's changes have little to do with our modern calendar. Solstices and equinoxes pass by unnoticed even though they affect our lives and the lengths of the days. There are other cycles as well, most of which also go unnoticed. We pass through puberty, the birth of a child, retirement, and old age with little recognition and celebration of those major changes. Yet we still continue to wonder why we feel no connection with the planet that nurtures us and the universe that contains us.

We are also disconnected from each other. At our home, we have a neighbor behind our house who does his best to make sure that he does not look our way when he walks his dog. Though I have tried many times to wave hello, I have been ignored. We feel no need to know even our next-door neighbors. There are cycles and connections between people and the other inhabitants of Gaia that also go unnoticed. (In this book, I will use the word *Gaia* to represent the living planet, and *Earth* will be the word for one of the four elements of the universe.) We have so many chances to celebrate our lives with each other and with the Great Mother that is the cosmos. If we do not recognize them, they pass us silently by and, as they do, we drift further and further apart from the very things that can help us feel renewed and connected. Pagans recognize the cycles of the world. So, living the Pagan life is both:

1. Learning to recognize these cycles and then making a commitment to honor them and live by them.

2. Using these cycles to help make improvements in our own lives and the world around us.

Within this book, I will take a look at the many different cycles of the universe and of life. Though we know that Gaia circles the sun, that the moon circles Gaia, and that the shadow of Gaia causes different light to appear on the moon, what our bodies experience is different and is the same thing that people have been experiencing for thousands of years. We observe a rising of the sun in the morning and a setting of the sun in the evening, when the moon then makes its appearance as it tracks across the night sky. We observe how it appears slightly different each night. We experience the seasons and the differing amounts of sunlight each day of the year. We experience Gaia cycles we call days as well as moon cycles that we call months, and cycles of the sun are labeled years. There are also life cycles. We all experience birth, puberty, adolescence, maturity, old age, and death. We will look at all these cycles and learn how to celebrate and honor them, and use them for the betterment of all.

1

Creating a Pagan
Way of Life

Introduction

You've studied Paganism. You've gone to rituals and you've taken classes. You're attracted to the freedom and self-determination that is a part of Pagan practice. But, somehow, it doesn't seem to be enough. Paganism is a frame of mind, an attitude, a way of living with the world and with each other that reflects Pagan principles. To be truly Pagan means to live your life in accordance with your Pagan understanding of the divine, the universe, the world, yourself, and others. When you have reached this type of understanding, you then come to ask yourself how this can be done. How can one create a lifestyle that truly reflects a Pagan understanding of life?

First, you must clearly understand what it means to be Pagan. This book is not an introduction to Paganism. There are already many great books on that topic, but I would like to mention what I think are the basic principles of Paganism. I call these principles the Pillars of Paganism.

The 3 Pillars of Paganism

1. All things are sacred, for the divine exists both within and beyond us.

2. We are free to choose our life and spiritual path and, consequently, are responsible for the choices we make.

3. We honor and celebrate the natural cycles of the universe.

The first statement is probably the most important and is what sets Paganism apart from most Western religions. With Paganism, there is no separation between the divine and the self, and yet there is an understanding that the divine is not just the self either. Spirit or the Ultimate Reality (or whatever term you use) is within us and beyond us because it is all things. We may honor deities but also know that, at the same time, we are also the essence of God or Goddess. We are all part of the greatness of being. As is often said in the Upanishads: Whatsoever you believe is holy, you are that, my friend, you are that. Within this text I will be using the term *Spirit* to denote the ultimate unifying energy in all beings and the universe. Please feel free to interject your own term wherever this term arises.

The second two statements follow from the first. Because we are part of the divine, we are endowed with a certain freedom to live our own life, to find our own path, and to respect the paths of others, for they are just as divine as we are. With that freedom, however, comes the understanding that we are responsible for our actions. We cannot blame what we do on a god or devil, for we are an equal part of divinity. We recognize our own freedom in the Rede (As it harm none, do as you will) that many Wiccans follow. This freedom means that we can take wisdom from wherever we may find it and develop a Pagan theology that is uniquely our own and that does not require all to believe or practice in the same way.

The final statement says that we are Gaia-centered because we celebrate the natural cycles of Gaia and the universe. We recognize the cycles of the moon and the sun, and we honor them as part of the deep mystery of all cycles that are part of life. Pagans most often celebrate these cycles through the practice of sacred rituals in which we directly participate in this cosmic dance.

Accepting, believing, and practicing these things in our lives creates a Pagan way of life. We commit ourselves to honoring the sacred in all things by the belief that all life and all things are sacred. We are free to choose our own path and understand that we must take the time and effort to devise our own way of celebrating the sacred rather than depending on someone else's pre-planned method. Even this book is no exception. I will not try to tell you the one and only way of making Paganism a way of life. Instead, I will offer several suggestions, but it will be up to you to determine your own practice. We learn to honor those cycles in our lives through the knowledge that the whole universe is sacred and reflects the beauty of the divine. By recognizing and honoring regularly the divine presence exhibited in natural cycles and in all life, we begin to develop a life that is truly spiritual and Pagan. Rituals and classes become only part of the many ways we connect to the universe and to each other. As we continue to practice, we develop a love of life and a desire to improve both our lives and the lives of others. We can develop practices that include honoring the sacred, self-improvement, and a commitment to serve others.

The challenge to leading a Pagan lifestyle is daily life itself. There are a thousand things that constantly call to us for attention. We have responsibilities and commitments. We have jobs, families, houses to keep up, lawns to mow, kitchens to clean, paperwork, homework, schoolwork, doctor appointments, dentist appointments, therapist appointments, soccer games, football games, hockey games, taxes, meetings, and memos—and I'm sure there are many other things you could add to this list. If all these things fulfill you, then I honor you and your joy. But for some people, living life this way is similar to eating a hamburger without the meat (or, in my case, without the veggie patty): You can take a big bite full of bread, lettuce, ketchup, and tomato, but you know there's something missing. Adding substance to a busy life can be challenging. It requires that you either find a way to make your life a little less busy or that you carefully manage your time to fit everything in—including spiritual sustenance. It also requires a promise to yourself. If it is really important to you that your life be lived spiritually and that it reflect your Pagan values, then you have to be willing to commit yourself to those practices that will do that. There are many things you can do to make your life more spiritual without adding large amounts of time to your schedule, but you may feel that it is important to carve out some blocks of time for spiritual practice so that you truly feel connected to your source of divinity and to the universe. This text will provide a plethora of ideas on how to do that, but how much you choose to do will, naturally, be up to you. Feel free to use as many of these ideas as you see fit.

The Cycles of the Universe

There are many cycles that surround us. Some we are aware of and others we are not—or at least most people are not. Pagans are usually the exception to that rule because we have committed ourselves to honoring Gaia. Let's take a close look at those cycles and how we experience their manifestations.

There are cycles of Gaia called *days*. Actually, these are cycles between Gaia and the sun or, more accurately, between the rotation of Gaia and the sun. Approximately every 24 hours, Gaia rotates on her axis, enabling different parts of her surface to be filled with the light and warmth of our solar system's sun (unless of course there are clouds or smog to block the way). The day's journey from light to dark affects everything we do. We are most active during the light part of the day and sleep through most of the night. Within every day there are certain things that happen. They, too, are part of the regular patterns of Gaia cycles and depend upon particular activities that we must do each and every day in order to stay alive. I remember as a child that I could not understand why we had to eat and sleep. All these things got in the way of letting me continue to play and imagine. Only much later in life did I realize what these things really are and why they are important to us. I believe that eating, sleeping, breathing, and engaging with others keeps us connected to Gaia and to all life. They are activities that remind us that we are not separate beings. We depend on Gaia—Her food, air, and creatures—to continue living because we are an integral part of the whole fabric of the life of Mother Gaia. We are Her and She is us. When we do these things we are reconnecting to Gaia and to the Spirit of the universe that is the source of all life.

To me, each of these daily requirements is a spiritual act worthy of respect and reverence, and we can live our lives in a way that reflects this adoration of the sacred in our life patterns. Many of our daily activities are related to these regular cycles of the day. For example, we all rise in the morning (unless you're in college, pulling an all-nighter), we all eat at least two to three meals per day (unless you're fasting or unable to obtain food), most of us go to a job or workplace (unless you've got a rich uncle), many of us return home after work, and most of us go to bed at night. These are things we do every day.

There are also weekly rituals. The week is actually a cycled relationship between Gaia and the moon. We divide the month or moon cycle of 28 days into four quarters, each with seven days we call the *week*. We can use the cycle of the week to engage in some activities that we may not want to do every day. Going to church on Sunday is a regular weekly ritual for many people. Some have meetings or practices on certain days of the week. There are people who see Wednesday as a day for midweek spiritual practices—a day for prayer meetings, Bible study, or choir rehearsals. Almost everyone has some kind of weekend ritual, such as going out to dinner on Friday night or watching the big game on Saturday.

There are cycles of the moon. The sun's light and the shadow of Gaia reflected on the moon changes the appearance of the moon. It appears to change from full light to complete darkness and then to full again approximately every 28 days. This moon cycle became known as the *month*. In ancient times, priests would determine when a month began by observing the moon. In ancient Rome, the first of the month was called the Calends, and from that we got the word *calendar.* Pagans celebrate the night of the full moon in a ceremony called an Esbat. Some also celebrate the dark moon in a celebration I have dubbed the Astor because it is the best time to see the stars.

There are also cycles of the sun. The time it takes for Gaia to return to any position in its orbit around the sun is called a *year.* Because the axis of Gaia is tilted in its relationship to the sun, various locations on its path around the sun allow certain parts of Gaia to receive more of the sun's light at particular times of the year. That influence is in opposition from the northern hemisphere of Gaia to the southern hemisphere. So, when the northern hemisphere receives the most light, the southern hemisphere receives the least. This amount of light and heat on the surface of our planet greatly affects our weather and our lives. These times are called the *seasons*, and we subdivide the year into four of them, which we call Winter, Spring, Summer, and Fall. The point at which the sun offers the greatest amount of heat and light in one hemisphere is known in that hemisphere as the Summer solstice; in the opposite hemisphere it is known as the Winter solstice. The points in between the two solstices, where light and dark are even, are known as equinoxes. Every year has two solstices and two equinoxes. Pagans celebrate these times of the year in order to recognize these changes and cycles, and to honor the cosmic forces that make them happen. Pagans also celebrate the times between the solstices and equinoxes, creating a total of eight solar holidays known as Sabbats.

Finally, there are also cycles in our lives that go beyond the single year. All life from birth to death is seen as a cycle because the death of one allows another to live and thrive. Within the cycles of birth and death are many changes that affect every human life. We can honor and celebrate those parts of the life cycle as well. Besides the event of being born, we also experience the time when we change from being a child to being an adult. Later, many people choose to get married or handfasted, or take on a life partner. Becoming pregnant and having a child are also life-changing events for all involved in the process. For women, menopause signals a shift to middle age. (For men, it may be a sudden desire to buy a small, red sports car.) We also experience a transition from middle age to becoming what is known as a *senior citizen*, when we might retire from years of work. Finally, we will all experience the end of our life cycle: death. These are regularly occurring cycles that affect every life. We often view our life in terms of a straight line because we are conscious only of our own birth and death, and not how each cycle of life affects the whole pattern of existence. If we could step back and see our life as part of the whole dance of the gods, we might also see our lives as part of a great cycle—just as the rise and fall of the sun and the moon. In the chart on page 27, I have compared the cycles of life to the patterns of the solar and lunar changes we observe. I call this chart the Wheel of Life.

The outer circle indicates the regular changes of the moon as it passes from full to dark every 14 days, and then from dark to full in the next 14 days. Similarly, our lives take on significant changes every 14 years. Around the age of 14, we make the transition from child to adult. At 28, we are on our way to becoming symbolic (or real) mother and father figures. This does not necessarily mean that we have our own children to raise, but we do begin to think about having a life partner, establishing a regular home life, and caring for others. Around 42, we hit the proverbial mid-life crisis, when we look back on our past and begin to assess the meaning of our lives and what our legacy will be to the world. This is often a life-changing time for many people, and understanding

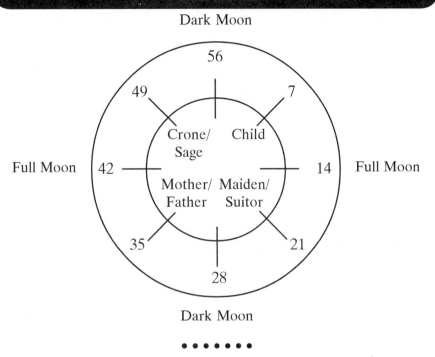

Wheel of Life

Dark Moon

56

49   7

Crone/   Child
Sage

Full Moon   42 — 14   Full Moon

Mother/ Maiden/
Father   Suitor

35   21

28

Dark Moon

• • • • • • •

that this is a normal transition in life can help it become less frightening and a more positive learning experience. In the stage of crone and sage, we can honor the wisdom we have gained from living a full life. People used to retire at 55, but many now delay retirement. Though it has become financially impossible for many to retire around the age of 55, there is still a sense of major transition at this time. It is a time when we feel the need to return to a childlike state of wonderment. Many people are still quite healthy at this age, making it a good time to begin a new sense of exploration. It is a chance to let go of life's responsibilities and embrace the beauty and wonders of the world. This is a time for playing with grandchildren, touring the country, or volunteering for causes that are important to you.

Now that you have identified your spiritual goals as a practicing Pagan and have observed the cycles of the universe and how they can be matched to those goals, you may be looking over everything and feeling a bit overwhelmed. There's a lot there to consider, and your life is already busy enough. This is the time to consider how much you can really commit to these goals and cycles. A religious practice must be as practical as it is enriching. I advise you not to fret, however. Though there may be quite a bit you want to add to your practice, you do not have to change everything all at once. In fact, you can slowly add to and change your practice as you go, which will also give you time to consider the reasons and effects you desire.

Reasons for Taking on This Work

The practice of Living Paganism may, at first, appear a bit daunting, so it might help to go over the reasons for beginning such a practice. Here are some reasons Pagans want to develop a more spiritual way of life based on Pagan values:

1. To develop a better quality of life.
2. To help determine what is truly important in life.
3. To feel more connected to Gaia, Spirit, and all beings.
4. To add magick and fun to life.
5. To feel and act truly Pagan within and beyond.

The first reason listed is about one's quality of life. When we do not leave time for seeking beauty, truth, the right, and the good; if we do not live to share joy with one another; if we do not live in a deep relationship with Spirit but live only to exist from one day to the next, there is no quality of life. Quality implies a fullness—a richness in something. There are those who have only the means to survive and who, for whatever reason, cannot pursue a greater quality of life. It is for that very reason that those of us who have the opportunity to do so must help those who cannot, for, as children of Spirit, we all deserve the chance to pursue this quality. For those who are capable of pursuing a better life, the first step is committing yourself to a spiritual practice that helps you find it and develop it. A higher quality of life comes from determining goals that allow you to live better, more spiritually, and in greater connection to yourself, others, and Gaia and Spirit.

By taking time to determine your spiritual goals and how you will meet them through the cycles, you force yourself to decide what is truly important to you in your life. This is an important act in and of itself. Too often, the busy pace of life does not allow us to take time out of life and consider the bigger questions of life. Considering what is truly meaningful to you in your life allows you to make decisions as to which things and practices need to be included and which need to be eliminated so that your life is lived closer to your values.

A Pagan spiritual practice also allows you to feel more connected to those cycles of the universe that we revere as sacred. As you work within these cycles, you will begin to feel as if you are a part of them rather then separated from them. We can ignore these cycles but we cannot truly be alienated from them, for they affect every part of our lives and the world in which we live. As we come closer to recognizing, celebrating, and moving within these cycles, we become an integral part of them and make it possible to live a healthier and more fulfilled life that recognizes and responds to the realities of life.

Pagans believe in magick and fun. I define magick as willful transformation. We have the capability to change our lives and the lives of others for the better. We do this change through our conscious will, which is defined by our intent. By determining your spiritual goals, you are defining your intent to live spiritually and within the natural cycles. You are also creating an intent to live more fully and with greater meaning and depth. Through this intent you direct your will to these goals and you begin to transform your life. This is indeed powerful magick. As you continue to grow, you develop the desire to help others. Thus, your transformation leads to the willful transformation of the lives of others. Again, this is great magick. When you intent is pursued through Spirit, your magick is infused with the powers of the universe, making it possible for great change. Part of magick, though, is also having fun. Unlike many of the Western religions, Paganism does not consider the body to be a detriment to spiritual practice. We celebrate the senses and the body's capacity to feel pleasure and ecstasy. These things are also part of the greatness and joy of Spirit. As long as harm is not intended, as long as a harmful addiction is not created, pleasure for pleasure's sake is not to be shunned. Following spiritual goals within the cycles of the universe can and should lead to fun as much as it does to serious reflection and contemplation. Leading a serious Pagan life is also joyful!

Finally, one of the best reasons to pursue this practice is because it is how we can truly act and feel Pagan. To be truly Pagan means to live within cosmic cycles and to worship them as sacred through our deities. Within ourselves we become Pagan when we feel the inner cycles of our bodies and how they are connected to the rhythm of the whole universe. By adding our own spiritual goals that honor these cycles and the deities we relate to them, we find our own way to worship the sacredness of these cycles and all the lives that are fulfilled through them. As we do this inner work, we begin to express our values through our outer selves. Others begin to see us as more focused and centered individuals. They will see our growing sense of connection and fulfillment. Hopefully, you will develop these things through your growing sacred practice and you will then spread this joy to others. The world needs a sense of connection to Gaia and to the universe, and you can begin to help the world reawaken this realization.

Developing a Pagan Practice Through the Cycles

We have observed the many cycles of life that influence our lives, and I have argued that learning to live a Pagan way of life involves honoring those cycles. How do we do that, though? Well, there are three steps that can help us learn to do that.

Steps for Developing a Practice

1. Determine your spiritual goals as a practicing Pagan.

2. Observe the cycles of the universe and of life, and develop a reverence for them.

3. Adopt practices based on your goals that honor and use these cycles.

Determining Goals

The first step to creating a life that reflects Pagan values and principles is to determine your own personal spiritual goals. To do this, you need to understand what a spiritual goal is and how it differs from any other kind of goal. A spiritual practice is anything that helps you deepen and further your connection to Spirit according to your theology. For many religions this means an intense development of interior exploration in such practices as prayer, meditation, or ritual work in order to connect with an outside force. These things are all important, but remember: Spirit is in all things. Pagan practice requires that we work to deepen our connection to Spirit both within ourselves and throughout the whole of the universe. Consequently, a true Pagan practice develops the connections of all relationships and strives to balance between them.

There are four realms of relationships that you need to consider when constructing a balanced practice: yourself, others, Gaia, and Spirit. Because Spirit is both within and beyond, your spiritual practice also needs to include the development of yourself. With these practices you work to develop the higher self through your Pagan values and ideals. This is where prayer, meditation, and ritual work have their proper place. With each practice, you are working to become a better person and Pagan practitioner as you connect to that deep part of yourself that is closest to Spirit. Furthermore, a true Pagan practice includes honoring the changes in life. As we live, learn, and grow, we change. Instead of fearing natural changes, we can learn to honor and celebrate them as part of the great ever-changing mystery of life.

That which is deep within you is also deep within all others (whether or not they act like it). When we find that part of Spirit that is inside us, we experience an intense sense of life, love, and peace, and we develop a desire to help others obtain the same. Those who suffer or are in need deserve the same chance to experience peace and happiness in their lives as we do. Part of spiritual practice, then, must include working to aid others. Doing these practices helps us to connect to another part of ourselves and to see the universal energy of Spirit that is in all beings. We must also commit ourselves to making a deeper connection to Gaia and all her sacred children, and to the mysterious essence of Spirit itself. We can do the former by developing practices that respect and honor Gaia as a living being and as a part of the greatness of Spirit, and we can do the latter by being open to the great mysteries and cycles of all life.

In all of these practices we must also consider the need for balance. Too often, spiritual practitioners focus on one area while disregarding others, causing a sense of imbalance that leads them to wonder what is missing in their spiritual life. A life dedicated solely to meditation without considering service to others and work for the environment can lead to a heightened sense of self-righteousness and a lack of deepened connections. That, of course, depends on your meditation practice. If such a practice leads to those other things because of an understanding of the mysterious connection of all beings, then it is a worthwhile practice. In my experience, the people whom I have most respected as greatly spiritual are those who have learned to incorporate all these things into their practice. So, all this is to say that we need to develop spiritual goals that are all-inclusive and balanced so that our Pagan lifestyle includes deepening connections to all our relationships.

Observing Cycles

To connect practices to natural cycles requires that you first carefully observe these cycles and notice their influence on your life. Having read this far in the book, you have already learned about those cycles. What I recommend you do next is simply take the next month or two and carefully take note of these cycles. Watch all the cycles of the day and how you react to them.

Begin by observing your own personal rituals and cycles. What do you normally do the first thing in the morning? What habits do you have around eating? What regular cycles exist at work and at home? What habits do you have regarding the evening and preparing for bed? You may also want to observe some of those things that you normally miss by doing the same thing every day. Then, observe the patterns involved with interacting with other people, yourself, and the world around you. Who do you see on a regular basis? What are your actions with them normally like? What people have an influence on them? Who do you see only once in a while or rarely? Which people feed your soul? Who drains you? Who have you not seen for a long time? Consider the people that help to brighten your day and your life. What things do you depend on being there every day? Then, observe the patterns of the people around you. What habits do they have? What cycles do they depend on (knowingly or unknowingly)?

Begin to observe the cycles of the celestial bodies around us. Take some time to just observe the rising and setting of the sun. Where does the sun mark its travels across the sky? What do the clouds do? From which direction does the wind usually blow? What happens when a storm is approaching? How do the plants and animals react to different weather conditions? What weekly cycles do you have? Which days of the week are more special and why? What are your weekday routines, and how do they compare with your weekend routines? Take some time to observe the moon. What does it really look like? How does its appearance change? Where does it travel across the sky at night? How does the light upon it change, and from which direction? What can you observe in the stars? What constellations can you identify? How do the stars change each night and through the year? These are just some of the many things you can notice about natural cycles with each day and night.

Although it is much more subtle, Spirit has changing cycles as well. To notice the cycles of Spirit, you need to develop a holistic sense of vision—to try and see the connection between all things and to notice changes in the overall pattern of things. Spirit seeks to stay in a state of change. To do this, it must continually move in cyclic and circular patterns. This activity appears to include an extending motion and a returning motion. In this text, I will refer to the extending motion as Expression, and the returning motion as Envelopment. I say that they appear to be this way because all the motions are really part of a single, unified pulsation. We can understand it the same way we understand that night and day appear to us to be times when the sun is turning its light on and off but, in reality, this only an illusion caused by the turning of Gaia. During the day, the light of the sun looks to us to be constant, but that is also an illusion. The sun itself is an endlessly changing storm of nuclear activity. The same is true of Spirit, whose energy is constantly changing, but whose existence as the source of life creates a sense of consistency. Life is the manifested state of Spirit and so must be in a state of constant flux as well. By observing larger patterns of change, we can observe the force of Spirit's Expressing and Enveloping, and we can also observe another important force of Spirit that is the need to constantly balance Expression with Envelopment.

I suggest you just take one month of your life to truly observe all these things, how they affect you, and how you feel about them. Use your journal book, or start one and make notes about each of these events in your life. It doesn't matter how much or how little you write—only that you engage fully in the act of observing the world around you.

Observation Worksheet

Date: _____

Moon phase: _____

Sunrise: _____

Sunset: _____

Weather: _____

How do you feel today?

Morning observation (self/others/Gaia/Spirit):

Noon observation (self/others/Gaia/Spirit):

Evening observation (self/others/Gaia/Spirit):

Night sky:

Interactions with people:

Observations of larger patterns of Expression, Envelopment, and Balance:

Other notes:

• • • • • • •

By carefully observing these cycles as well as the larger cycles of the sun and of life, we can begin to take the second step toward developing a Pagan lifestyle: developing a reverence for the sacred patterns of the universe. If you recall the first of the 3 Pillars of Paganism, you will be reminded that Pagans believe that all things are sacred. The divine exists within and beyond all things. It is the source of all that is and reveals itself through its manifestation, which we call life. The constantly changing expression of the source is what we recognize as these cycles. Therefore, we recognize these cycles as all being of divine origin. If you have taken a month to really observe these cycles, you have done more than most people do in years. If you can then see these cycles as part of the divine life patterns of the universe and as a revelation of Spirit, then you will do more than most people do in their lifetimes. If you observe the intricate workings of the cosmos and of our lives within those patterns it will be hard for you not to be awed by the divine mystery of it all. This sense of awe is the first step toward developing a feeling of reverence for the cosmos and the magick energies within it. There are some simple ways to develop reverence of these cycles. For example, you could stop and see what things you may have missed on your way to work or find the hidden things of beauty that are around your house. Take a chance to truly taste your food rather than hurry through a meal before your next appointment. Take a few minutes in the morning and evening to appreciate the quiet (if possible) or the darkness. Learn to appreciate the weather every day, as well as the surprises and changes it brings.

Incorporating Goals Within Cycles

The final step in developing a Pagan lifestyle is to adopt practices that honor and incorporate those sacred cycles. When you do this, you pay tribute to the great mystery of life, and you become consciously aware and begin to live within its cycles. Through this way of living, you learn to appreciate all life and seek to develop ways to improve yourself and the world around you. These practices come in the form of how you approach your activities, through sacred ritual used to mark certain cycles and occasions, and through small acts of devotion done throughout the day and at certain times within those cycles. This may seem to be a daunting list of things to add to one's life, but when you become conscious of the sacredness of life and how you can honor that sacredness, you find ways of slowly adding these things to your routines until they become an integral part of your life.

Once you have come to observe and incorporate the meaning of the cycles into your life, you can then begin to determine which cycles are best for helping you meet your spiritual goals. Some of the practices you develop will be best done at certain times of the day, or on certain days of the week, or on certain days of the year. Each of these times intersects with different cycles. You can determine which goals will need to be connected with which cycles. Then, as you follow these cycles in your life as a practicing Pagan, you will also be able to meet your own spiritual goals and begin to develop yourself as a truly spiritual person.

2

Determining
Spiritual Goals

Introduction

In this chapter we'll take a look at a wide variety of possible methods for developing a spiritual practice for self, others, Gaia, and Spirit. The beginning of each section will list a set of general goals. This list will help you refer back to these sections when you begin to synthesize your goals with the sacred cycles. Within each section, you can choose those practices that resonate best with you, and then organize them together into your own spiritual program. At the end of each section is a short list of questions designed to help you identify those goals that you determine you would like to make part of your spiritual practice. After reading each section, take a few minutes to answer the questions on a separate piece of paper or in your journal. At the conclusion of the chapter, you can put them all together and create a chart of spiritual goals.

Each section will list possible goals in relation to the four elements (Earth, Air, Fire, and Water) and the three energies of all cycles (Expression, Envelopment, and Balance) through four sets of relationships (Developing the Self, Helping Others, Honoring Earth and Spirit, and Honoring Yourself and Others).

Practices for Developing the Self

General goals for developing the self:

▷ Physical Expression.

▷ Physical Envelopment.

▷ Mental Expression.

▷ Mental Envelopment.

▷ Emotional Expression.

▷ Emotional Envelopment.

▷ Soulful Expression.

▷ Soulful Envelopment.

Spiritual development must begin with developing the spiritual needs of the self. You cannot help others or seek a deeper connection to Spirit if you are not yourself capable of these things. To develop the self, you must seek wholeness by taking care and strengthening each part of the self. We will look separately at each of the four parts of self—body, mind, heart, and soul—and observe practices that can be used to strengthen each for spiritual practice. We will also discuss those things that call to each part of self and pull them toward Spirit. Spirit is the source of all energy. It is the source of what makes us alive and unique, and is the source of all that we seek. As with the statue of the dancing Shiva whose dance must continue for all to live, the dance of Spirit is eternal. This constant motion creates the cycles we experience in all things. That energy manifests through us in a force called Life. Each practice concerning self and others must balance the forces of the motion of Expressing and Enveloping. The force of Expression gives us the strength to be ourselves, whereas Envelopment calls us to come together. Our lives are in constant motion between the need to express our individuality and the need to enfold our unity. To be healthy and vibrant we must allow each of these needs to be fulfilled. Wisdom allows us to carefully balance these needs. The following chart lists the four parts of the self, their relation to the elements, and how each can experience Expression, Envelopment, and Balance.

ELEMENT	EARTH	AIR	FIRE	WATER
PART	Physical	Mental	Emotional	Soulful
EXPRESSION	Movement	Speaking truth	Living the good	Living the right
ENVELOPMENT	Seeking beauty	Seeking truth	Seeking the good	Seeking the right
BALANCE	Rest	Silence	Peace	Tolerance

Each part of us seeks to express itself to others and to the universe, and also seeks to embrace and return to Spirit by finding the greatest representations of Spirit, which we experience as beauty, truth, good, and right in the world and in others. Now, I am perfectly aware that not all people are full of goodness and light. There have been and always will be those who seek to cause harm and whom we may label as evil for the harm they do cause. I would argue, however, that even those people we label as "evil" desire to express and experience Spirit. It is just that good and right for them are expressed in harmful ways. That is why practices of self must always be balanced with the effects and consequences of those practices on self, other, Gaia, and Spirit, and the need for Expression must be balanced by the need for Envelopment. It is not selfish to want to desire to develop yourself to your fullest potential, but it is selfish if you do so without any consideration for allowing all others to do the same. It is also not selfish to want to love and be loved as long as you realize these two things must go hand in hand. Be honest about your own needs and develop practices that help you obtain those needs in a truly balanced way.

Practices for Self: Earth

The element Earth relates to the body. The body expresses through motion and is enveloped through beauty. Methods of Expression for the body are strenuous motion, relaxed motion, and through touching. Methods of Envelopment are experienced through seeking pleasure, living in natural beauty, and through being active in the arts. Balance is found by seeking rest.

The body needs to move or it becomes useless. Every doctor and health manual will stress the importance of giving the body some strenuous exercise in order to maintain good health. At the very least, 20 minutes a day, three to five days a week should be spent on some type of active exercise to help keep the body moving and functioning. One of the best and safest forms of exercise is walking, which is also a great way to get out of our unnatural environments and connect back to nature. It is important to find a form of exercise that you enjoy or you will not stick with it. If walking or jogging is not your thing, consider taking up some kind of game or sport that helps keep your body moving. Some enjoy exercising alone; others need to be in a group to have fun and find encouragement to continue. Another possible way to find some exercise is to take a weekly class that involves moving. This could include activities such as aerobics, martial arts, or dance classes. The body can also move through less strenuous exercises, which need to be done more often to get the same benefit or, better yet, should be combined with some form of active exercise. Less-strenuous exercise can be found through practices such as yoga, gardening, and movement activities such as t'ai chi or chi kung.

There are also simple ways to let your body express itself. You can become more conscious of the way your body appears throughout the day. How do you move? Does your body express itself as tired and uncomfortable with itself, or can people see a vibrancy of life in each step you take? How does your body move through the day? How do your hands move? How do you carry yourself? Let your body express on the outside the joy and sense of wonder you have on the inside (which you will develop through your spiritual practices).

Our bodies seek the beautiful as a way to return to the purity of Spirit, and the beautiful is sought through the senses. We seek pleasure, and Pagans believe that seeking and finding pleasure is a wonderful thing so long as harm is not caused to another. We do not believe that we should disregard the need to have pleasurable experiences as long as balance is also sought, but the strong pull of the desire for pleasure can lead to obsession and abuse. The right of seeking pleasure also comes with the responsibility of observing who and what is affected by seeking it. Through our five (some would say six) senses, we can experience the many pleasures of natural beauty as well as the wonderful works created through the hands of our fellow men and women. As Pagans, we realize the importance of communing with nature as much as possible. I, myself, find it difficult to remain indoors for any extended length of time. Through taking walks, going camping and hiking, going on picnics in the park, or playing outside, we can remain connected with the natural beauty of the world.

Our bodies need to experience the world through our senses, and it is through these experiences that we feel alive. We need to take time to literally smell the roses. Again, it is not selfish to take time out of your life to smell, taste, touch, hear, and see the world. Whenever you encounter a beautiful smell, take a few moments to actually enjoy it and the sensations that arise within you before moving on. When eating, instead of gulping down a meal, take some time to enjoy the wonderful flavors that fill your tongue. Enjoy the act of touching as well. Enjoy sex as a sacred act in which bodies are allowed to mingle and experience complete touch. Give and receive massages often to those who allow you to do so and, by all means, hug each other as much as you can. Take time to listen to the multitude of sounds around you. Listen to beautiful music or make your own. Enjoy the sound of another person's voice as he or she speaks to you. Take time also to see the many wondrous and beautiful things that exist everywhere in this world.

Seeking to balance the energies of Expression and Envelopment of the body comes through seeking rest. Our society so often demands that we work beyond our limits. This is unhealthy and detrimental to your own growth and to the way you share energies with others. Find time and ways to seek rest.

Exercise 1: The Body

Consider your answers to the following questions. I've provided space here for your answers, or you can write them in your journal or some other study guide.

1. What goals do you have for the spiritual Expression of the body through:

    Strenuous moving?

    _____

    _____

    _____

    Relaxed moving?

    _____

    _____

    _____

    Daily movements of the body?

    _____

    _____

    _____

2. What goals do you have for the spiritual Envelopment of the body
    by:

    Seeking the beautiful through taste?

    _____

    _____

    _____

    Seeking the beautiful through touch?

    _____

    _____

    _____

    Seeking the beautiful through smell?

    _____

    _____

    _____

    Seeking the beautiful through hearing?

    _____

    _____

    _____

    Seeking the beautiful through vision?

    _____

    _____

    _____

3. How will you balance these energies through seeking rest?

_____

_____

_____

_____

Practices for Self: Air

Just as the body needs to be in motion, the mind needs to learn and communicate in order to remain alive. The mind Expresses through communicating to others and through practicing wisdom. It finds Envelopment to Spirit through learning and listening, and by seeking the truth. Balance is sought through finding time for silence.

The mind is constantly filled with thoughts, and the way to express those thoughts to others is through communication. Most of us are in constant communication with ourselves, our friends, our lovers, and with a host of others in our lives. We often do not consider those communications as spiritual, but I believe that they are spiritual. Whether through our voices or in writing, if we take time to ponder the idea that the energies behind our thoughts come from Spirit, then we will realize the tremendous weight and power our conversations and writings have upon ourselves and others. Words are symbols of symbols, but are symbols nonetheless. Symbols are a powerful way of communicating, and care must be taken to ensure that the meaning implied through the symbols is the meaning we intend.

Intention, of course, is the key. We might ask ourselves before every conversation: What is the intent behind the words, and is that intent being made clear with the words I am using? So many problems arise from

47

people not being clear in their intent or by not asking others to make their intent clear as well. The solution for most interpersonal misunderstandings is in taking the time to speak openly and honestly about the feelings and intentions involved in the matter. Carefully observe how you speak to others. Sometimes it is a good practice to breathe deeply and fully before speaking. This can allow you to focus your intent before you begin and to speak from a calm place in your heart. This can be especially helpful when communicating to a person with whom you have had difficult dealings in the past. Unless you wish to unleash the full power of your anger (which can be an effective tool if used sparingly), speaking calmly will keep you from saying anything you might regret later. This does not mean you should not defend yourself. You could also demand from others that you will not speak to them until they first speak calmly to you. You are under no obligation to respond to the anger of another person. It is equally important to consider the same things when communicating with yourself. If you consistently put yourself down or belittle your abilities, you are engaging in a negative form of conversation. If you wish to live spiritually, you will realize the importance of speaking with respect to others and will insist on the same respect for yourself.

Another method of Expression for the mind is through the display of wisdom. Wisdom is different than knowledge and learning. Learning is obtaining, storing, and retrieving information, but wisdom is being able to take the information learned and apply it in ways that help you make good decisions and improve the conditions of yourself and all things. One who has wisdom is able to see things clearly and as they really are rather than through the smoky lens of a particular desire or need to manipulate. One who has wisdom can discern the true causes of actions and can accurately identify the possible consequences of those actions upon others.

One who is wise sees through the false trappings created by others to the stark reality of a situation. Most of all, one who is wise knows that not all things can be known and that all human knowledge is limited. The wise express their wisdom through careful observation and by relaying what they have learned to those who seek it. They never try to force their thoughts on others, for they know that doing so never leads to learning. All people must discover on their own or through their own volition. But where do the wise find their answers? They find them from seeking out other wise people, from learning wherever and whenever they can, and from observing and being with nature. They find them in the midst of silence and solitude, where they commune with their higher selves and with the wisdom of the gods and the universe. They find them by carefully observing the lessons of life and death. The wise know that lessons can be learned from everything we do, from everyone we meet, and from everywhere we go if we can be patient enough to look, listen, and learn the lessons.

The mind seeks to return to Spirit through learning and listening. There are many ways to learn, but all of them contain the prerequisite of having an open mind. There is a story of a master who encounters an arrogant student who believes that he already has all the answers. The student had approached the teacher, not to learn, but to have his beliefs confirmed. He had hoped to impress the teacher with his great knowledge. The teacher immediately recognized the difficulty in trying to reach this hardheaded student. After talking for several minutes, the teacher instructed the student to get him some tea. The student agreed and asked the teacher for his cup. The wise master grabbed his cup and gave it to the student, who took it and began to head toward the tea when he noticed that the cup was already full of tea. The neophyte turned back to the teacher and said, "Master, I cannot get you some tea, for your cup is already filled." The eyes of the teacher twinkled as he turned toward the student and replied, "As it is with you, my young one. A full cup cannot be filled with tea, and a full mind cannot learn." The wise know that they can never completely know and, thus, leave their minds always open to learn more.

With an open mind, you can begin to allow yourself to let knowledge and information in. A common method of learning, of course, is through the communications of others. You can read books, go to lectures, talk to others, see movies and art shows, surf the Net, or participate in other forms of communication. To try to reach Spirit, however, you need to include sacred teaching—the reading of sacred books and other methods of sacred learning. Pagans do not have a central text from which they are expected to get all their learning and inspiration. I think this is a good thing, because it frees us to read all sacred works and to be inspired by learning many different traditions. As members of a mystical religion, we understand that it is the relationship to the divine that is more important than the stories and the lessons that help us find that relationship. Having said all that, though, there is one sacred text that is important to all Pagans, but which is often overlooked. That text is not read through words or pictures; it is experienced and studied through participation. That sacred text is nature and Gaia herself. We can learn to read the lessons of Mother Earth by carefully observing Her and our relationship to Her. We can watch Her children play and live. We can commune with the trees and plants. We can listen to the wisdom of a waterfall or observe the waves of the ocean. We can gaze at the marvels in the sky that present themselves every day and every night. All these things can teach us about the mysteries of living just as well as any book or lecture.

We can also seek truth and learning by a particularly favorite method for Pagans: divination. To divine means literally to connect to the divine in order to access information that can help us. Divination allows you to use the powerful forces of chance and symbolism to reach parts of your unconscious and, consequently, Spirit to help you see things you may not have considered before. This is the act of seeking greater wisdom. Through tarot cards, runes, interpreting dreams, or other divination systems, the cosmic force of chance or chaos is allowed to act through the tools of that system. As you shuffle and select the particular tools, you enact the process of arranging chaos into order. These are basic powers of the universe, and they can help you seek great wisdom. Each system also uses a great variety of symbols that act directly to the unconscious symbolic part of our minds. Connecting different symbols to find their relationship and meaning also helps you discover greater wisdom.

An important part of learning and a method all its own to help the mind reach Spirit is through simply enhancing our ability to listen. In conversing with others, many people do not listen to each other with a truly open mind. Instead, discussions become similar to a tennis match where each person simply waits his or her turn to hit the ball—in this case, to talk about him or herself. To continue with the sports analogies, the good listener is closer to a baseball catcher: The catcher waits patiently to receive what the pitcher directs at him. Occasionally, the catcher offers suggestions and always brings the ball back into play. A good conversation, of course, means being able to take turns being the catcher and the pitcher. Sometimes, we also need to use the same skills we develop when we listen to others and apply them to listening to ourselves. Sometimes, when we are about to learn something about ourselves, we cut ourselves off so that we do not experience any pain. By being patient and open to ourselves, we allow ourselves the chance to learn about who we are and what we really need. We can also listen to the wisdom of the universe by embracing solitude when we need it. Too often, people are afraid of being alone because they fear the truth that may be revealed in those moments. Being alone with silence should not be feared. It is in times of solitude that we can truly learn about important things. By yourself, you can learn the secrets of the universe.

To balance the energies of Expression and Envelopment, you will need to also embrace silence. Some people, when they are together, will do anything to fill moments of silence. Some are uncomfortable with silence. A TV or radio may be left on all the time to fill that perceived void of sound. Some must be constantly engaged in conversation, but silence is an important tool for spiritual development. Two techniques for finding silence of the mind are meditation and the use of mantras.

One of the primary goals of meditation is to silence the mind so that it can be open to experience and learn new things. You do not have to sit in uncomfortable positions and make strange humming sounds to learn to be able to open the mind in silence. All it takes is a commitment to be open and to listen, to clear the mind and the environment of all distractions, and to concentrate on the silence itself. An easy technique is to simply sit comfortably and follow the breath as it moves through the body. Imagine that you are breathing with your entire body and feel yourself rise and fall gently with the breath. When your mind begins to drift, simply (without judging yourself) return to the sound and feeling of your breathing. Try to do this for one minute at first, and then gradually increase the amount of time until you can meditate for at least 20–30 minutes.

Another technique for quieting the mind used by many religious traditions is the use of a mantra. A mantra is a word or phrase that is repeated either audibly or silently. The purpose is to stop all the chatter within your head as you focus upon the phrase. Continuous repetition of the phrase creates an almost hypnotic effect over time that lets you relax and slow down your thoughts. This can create a sense of inner peace and calm. As you practice this technique more often, that inner serenity will come more quickly and more often. A mantra can be done almost anywhere and anytime, and can be especially useful in times when you are idle, such as when you have to wait in line or are in a traffic jam. To do this practice, simply find a word or short phrase that relates to your Pagan values or that can easily make you feel calm and connected to the peace of Spirit and the universe.

Exercise 2: The Mind

Consider your answers to the following questions. I've provided space here for your answers, or you can write them in your journal or some other study guide.

1. What goals do you have for the spiritual Expression of the mind through:

   Truthful communication?

   _____

   _____

   _____

   _____

   _____

Developing wisdom?

_____

_____

_____

_____

Expression through the senses?

_____

_____

_____

_____

2. What goals do you have for the spiritual Envelopment of the mind through:

Learning?

_____

_____

_____

_____

Listening?

_____

_____

_____

_____

3. What goals do you have for seeking Balance of the mind?

_____

_____

_____

_____

Practices for Self: Fire

The element Fire relates to the heart. The heart expresses through creativity and is enveloped by seeking the good. The heart remains in motion by experiencing different feelings and then communicating those feelings. We can say that doing so is speaking from the heart and that living openly with the self and others is living from the heart. When the heart speaks to others through its own language of symbols, we call that creativity. The heart is called to Spirit by embracing (physically or symbolically) the whole of creation. This, of course, starts by embracing the self, and then learning to embrace all others and all beings. Balance of the heart comes from finding inner and outer peace.

We spend most of our efforts at communicating by talking to one another and to ourselves. What you say and, more importantly, how you say it reflects upon who you are and what you believe. When you speak from the outer rim of daily desires and frustrations, you might come to express yourself from a place of control or hurt. You then send this energy out to others and, as does the ripple in the proverbial pond, that energy moves out to others and creates a wave of resentment and anger. If, instead, you can speak from a calm, centered place—from the true heart of the self—you can learn to interact peacefully. Our self-center is akin to the hub of a spinning wheel: it moves little and remains focused while the outer rim moves much faster. Speaking from the self's center is speaking from the heart. The heart speaks with compassionate truthfulness. Being compassionately truthful means speaking the truth without causing harm and may even lead one to occasionally lie if that is necessary to prevent further harm. As with all things, the difference lies in the intent. Our intent needs to be focused on revealing the truth so that it can further the right; but when there is no right to be gained, then we must consider the possible consequences of that truth. A right intent can only come from being honest with yourself about your desires and your feelings. With every action, we must consider what it is that we seek through that action and why. By being honest with our own feelings, we may come to learn that we are not as pure as we had hoped, but this is part of honesty. It is better to know this than to pretend it is not true. Only when you know the truth behind your actions can you begin to change them. Without this kind of personal observation, we can create patterns of pain and confusion when we find ourselves hurting others and then not knowing why.

One way in which we often hurt others is through our conversations. Talk that is hurtful is just as dangerous to yourself and to others as is physical harm. Harm can be caused physically, mentally, emotionally, and spiritually with equal damage. You may feel that hurting others through your words will help you obtain revenge, power, or control over others—and indeed it might for a time, but rarely is that feeling satisfying for a long time. As is true with all conflict, those who are hurt will simply return the energy by seeking to hurt in revenge. This is how arguments begin. This is how wars begin. Instead of searching for opportunities to hurl insults or establish your reputation over others, speaking from the heart offers you a chance to make the world just a tiny bit more humane.

On special days, Tibetan Buddhist monks will spend hours and hours filling tiny votive candles with butter and then lighting them throughout the temple. They may fill thousands of these small lights throughout the day, and it may take many hours to complete the task, but when they are done and the candles are all lit, the temple is awash in a beautiful golden display of light that can be seen for miles. We, too, can use our speech to either throw stones or light tiny candles. We can offer light by looking for opportunities to offer thanks and praise to others and to ourselves. This means more than just thanking people for what they have done for you; this involves actively seeking chances to praise and thank those who are doing small acts of goodness throughout the day.

Besides learning to speak from the heart, we can also learn to live from the heart. Living from the heart requires us to know who we are and then live our lives so that we can best reflect that true self. This is known as living authentically. To be authentic is to be honest about who you are to yourself and others. Again, intention is the key. If you can be aware of what your intent is for each action you wish to take, you can check that intention against the person you truly wish to be. We are defined by others through our actions, not our thoughts, but our thoughts and intentions guide what we do. In this way, our living becomes an act of expressing our true selves. This is living authentically.

Sometimes, though, some desire to express themselves more fully, and a deep desire to communicate thoughts and feelings to others in a more concrete way emerges. That type of Expression can be done through creativity. When one is creative, a tangible work (a work of art) is produced that expresses that person's unique viewpoint on a subject. Unfortunately, our society makes a distinction between amateur and professional artists. This can lead to a devaluing of the creator with less talent and experience, and can cause some to abandon any efforts to try to create anything at all for fear that their work will not be "good enough." Any expression that comes from the heart, however, is worth something to its creator, regardless of its possible value to others. That does not mean you should not share your ideas and creations with others, but it does mean you should keep in mind why you produced it in the first place. A work of art can be created by you and be only for you if that is your need or desire.

Creations and expressions of the heart can come in many forms. A tried-and-true spiritual practice of Expression is the writing of a journal. Most people know that journals are practices primarily done for the self and not shared with others. This freedom allows you to express yourself however you like without worry of review and criticism. Through a journal, you can mark your progress on your spiritual path through life. You can record practices and activities that have helped you grow as well as those that have not. Through your writing, you can let out deep and painful feelings as well as your most intense joys. Keeping a journal allows you to look back over your past and see your own story develop. Journals do not only need to be done through writing. Collections of drawings, photographs, sounds, or other mementos can create a significant record of events. There are many other methods of creative expression. The heart can express itself through visual art, photography, music, dance, literature, theater, and film. These are the traditional arts, of course, but there are also even more ways to find Expression, such as through cooking, gardening, flower arranging, building things such as unique cars or furniture, decorating your workplace, or decorating the house.

The heart seeks to know Spirit by seeking the good in the self and others. When we embrace Spirit, whether literally or figuratively, we are coming close to returning to Her. Our souls cannot truly return to Spirit until we die, but, by taking time to return to Her through our hearts, we will be reminded of who we really are: unique expressions of the whole. We will also learn to not fear death, because we will experience that to which we shall return.

To seek Spirit through the heart, we begin by embracing ourselves. We can do this by developing and increasing our own sense of self-worth. If you cannot value your own self, you will place little value upon your sense of purpose, upon your actions, and upon your interactions with others. I have advised many different students over the years. More often than not, the central issue in many of their lives was their lack of self-worth. We must come to recognize that there is no scale of value for all beings. We begin life the same way and with the same full blessing of Spirit from which we came. One tree is no less a tree than any other. Though trees come in different varieties, shapes, colors, sizes, and forms, none of these qualities determines the intrinsic value of the tree itself. Other humans may place a priority of worth upon trees, but the trees themselves have no such gradation of value. The same is true of all beings. One flower is no less a flower than another. All birds possess the same essence of being a bird. One human is no less than another. I am not speaking about whether or not a person is more good or bad than another. I am talking about the inner worth and pride of each person. Knowing this truth, you can begin to live out your life as an equally valued individual. You can begin to value what you do and not be afraid to connect with others. When you learn to value yourself, then you learn to recognize the same inherent worth of all others. Learning to embrace yourself, you come to understand the need to embrace others.

Balance of the heart's needs is sought through finding inner peace and then extending that peace to others. This may have to be found by silencing or working to overcome excessive anger or hatred that may be deep within you. If this is a serious problem for you, you may need to find people or sources who can help you resolve these things so that there can be room in your heart for this kind of peace. You cannot live peace or be at peace with others if you are not also at peace with yourself. Find this peace as a favor to yourself. You will come to be happier and others will also enjoy being in your company.

Exercise 3: The Heart

Consider your answers to the following questions. I've provided space here for your answers, or you can write them in your journal or some other study guide.

1. What goals do you have for the spiritual Expression of the heart through:

    Speaking from the heart?

    _____

    _____

    _____

    Living from the heart?

    _____

    _____

    _____

2. What goals do you have for the spiritual Envelopment of the heart through:

Embracing the self?

_____

_____

_____

Embracing others?

_____

_____

_____

3. What goals do you have for Balancing the heart?

_____

_____

_____

_____

Practices for Self: Water

The element Water relates to the soul. The soul expresses itself through our character and is attracted to the right. The soul remains in motion by living well and by living right. The soul seeks Spirit by always searching for answers and by applying wisdom, and seeks balance through tolerance and living in harmony with others.

The soul is the small spark of Spirit that lives within all beings. It is what makes each of us unique while also being part of the greater whole.

It is expressed by living fully and well. Living well begins by each of us having an understanding of our place in our own life, in the lives of others, and in the universe. This is a spiritual understanding and an important part of your Pagan practice. As you continue to understand that your purpose in life is to seek Spirit and to be a full participant in the dance of life, you can begin to live your life as it was meant to be lived. One practice to help you do this is to always be observant and open to the changes and wonders of life. Another is to learn to live spontaneously and joyfully. Life will always be full of challenges, for that is also part of the dance, but by focusing only on overcoming those challenges, you may miss some of the small joys that may come your way. It will always be necessary to overcome our difficulties, but we also need to make an effort to seek out joy.

Expressing through the soul also involves living rightly. All religious traditions insist that living spiritually involves espousing some form of what we call the Golden Rule or set of spiritual ethics. Living right is not something we do just because that is what our mothers taught us or because that is what we learned in kindergarten. Living rightly ensures a just and peaceful society where people can live together in harmony. If people were allowed to do whatever they wanted, whenever they wanted, and to whomever they wanted, there would be only chaos. People would have to spend their time forever living in fear and worrying about being under attack. Others would spend their precious time plotting new methods of revenge and plunder to replace all that was taken from them. Living rightly in the Pagan sense is to define for yourself a personal set of ethics that reflects your spiritual values, and then to live those values every day.

You can also learn to live the right by constantly reminding yourself of your values and being able to reassess them as you continue to learn and grow with them. Just deciding on a set of values once and then putting them away in some dark corner of your mind is not enough to live rightly. You must be willing to constantly remind yourself of those values and learn to apply them to every situation in which you might find yourself. Consequently, you may find that your ethical principles may need to be updated or refined as you continue to practice them.

The soul comes to Spirit by seeking the right. The right can only be sought by always asking questions and by trying to find the truth regardless of where it leads. We can ask questions audibly or within the mind, of course, but there are other ways to ask questions as well. We can contact Spirit through techniques such as dreamwork, pathworking, divination, aspecting deity, meditation, or other techniques. Through these methods, we reach out to a source of wisdom beyond our own in order to find answers. Paradoxically, another way to seek the right is to not actively seek answers. Sometimes it is necessary to clear the mind and simply wait for an answer. We can learn to simply be in the moment, every moment, and trust that answers will come to us when they are needed.

I consciously put soul last in the list of developments of the self, because accessing the soul really requires combining all the other parts of the self. The soul seeks Spirit when the body, mind, and heart are also in line to seek Spirit. We act, we think, and we feel our way to Spirit through the soul. We learn and then we apply that learning to living a full life. This is how you can learn to apply wisdom to create a meaningful and authentic life.

Balance for the soul is found by seeking tolerance through a respect for all beings. Tolerance is sought through the understanding that not everyone is going to be to your liking. It is in knowing that all people have a basic natural worth, endowed to them through Spirit, that exists in all beings and is worthy of respect.

Exercise 4: The Soul

Consider your answers to the following questions. I've provided space here for your answers, or you can write them in your journal or some other study guide.

1. What goals do you have for the spiritual Expression of the soul through:

Living well?

_____

_____

_____

_____

Living right?

_____

_____

_____

_____

2. What goals do you have for the spiritual attraction of the soul through:

Seeking answers?

_____

_____

_____

_____

Applying wisdom?

_____

_____

_____

_____

3. What goals do you have for Balance of the soul?

_____

_____

_____

_____

Practices for Self: Seeking Overall Balance

We have looked over things that can be done to develop parts of the self individually, but it is important to also keep our eye on the total picture. Developing one part of the self more than another can lead to an unhealthy imbalance. In all things, it is important to seek balance. That is the nature of the universe. Energy seeks to be in motion and to change but always through balancing its motions. In school we learned that energy is neither created nor destroyed. There can never be a surplus of one form of energy or another in total. We, too, need to seek such balance. What are the qualities of a balanced person? Such a person would recognize all the parts of herself and her relationship to all others, and seek a middle way between her needs and desires. Overall balance is sought by not emphasizing one part of the self over another. Look over your previous list of goals and notice whether some areas are emphasized more than others. If so, seek some ways to find balance.

Practices for Helping Others

General goals for helping others:

▷ Physical aid.

▷ Mental aid.

▷ Emotional aid.

▷ Spiritual aid.

Any practice that focuses on the needs of the self while disregarding the needs of others cannot be truly spiritual. We need to become strong and independent people if we are to help others—it's true. You must help the self before you can help others, but developing the self is only part of the energy that creates the constant cycles of life. You can satisfy needs and desires and gain a sense of self-value through this satisfaction, but you will never feel connected if you do not also consider the needs and desires of others. One who is compassionate is not weak. You can learn to defend yourself, be assertive, and stand your ground while also learning to help others be strong as well. In fact, it takes more strength and courage to be both confident and compassionate. You can learn to balance your needs with the needs of others, but it takes energy, skill, and a willingness to cooperate and negotiate. If we take on this work together, we then create a more just and open society. If Spirit is that which is within and beyond us, then helping others is a spiritual act. By working with those who are in need or by working for the betterment of Gaia, we become part of the process of healing. In doing so, we also uplift and improve ourselves. It is a well-known fact that helping others helps the self. Our own suffering appears small in the light of all the suffering of others, but continuing to add negative energy to the world only lengthens the suffering of all. When you put forth positive energy into the world, it will in time work its way back to you.

ELEMENT	EARTH	AIR	FIRE	WATER
PART	Physical	Mental	Emotional	Soulful
AID	Helping to provide physical needs	Valuing others; offering education	Loving and helping to feed others	Providing spiritual support

Just as you can develop the self through the elements, you can use these same elements to help others. Through the development of the self, you strengthen your body, mind, heart, and soul, and in helping others you can do the same for them. You can respect and promote others through the development of their bodies, minds, hearts, and souls. In that way, you help the whole person and not just a part of him or her. You can also respect that others have the same energy and blessings that came from the single source of all: Spirit. Just as you draw upon that energy to express yourself through the force of Expression, so do others have that same need. And just as you are also called back to the energy of the universe through the force of Envelopment, we must remember that all other beings have that same urge to come together. You can honor these basic truths by respecting others in their need to express themselves and by working to care and love others. This is hard work because it calls us to go beyond simply caring for ourselves in disregard of the needs of others, but that is the calling of the spiritual person.

Practices for Helping Others: Earth

When most people think of helping others, they think first about the body. We live in a physical world and we all have physical needs that we must fulfill every day. Some are fortunate enough to be supported by others or can support themselves. Unfortunately, not everyone is so lucky. Poverty, hunger, and homelessness have been with us for a long time and will probably not be eradicated in the near future. The reasons for the existence of these problems are complex and are intertwined with our culture, politics, and attitudes. They are not problems that can be explained away simply by saying things such as "those people don't work hard enough" or "those people just don't care." Few people choose to be homeless, and most would be willing to work if given an opportunity and training. Changing these problems can only happen through a combined effort, but there are still things you can do as a compassionate individual. You can work with local agencies that help to clothe and house others. You can donate money and/or time to good causes. Each small bit of help can make a difference in the lives of others.

Working in the service of others does not have to involve long hours at a volunteer center or moving to a third-world country, however. Though these things are beneficial, there are simple things that can be done every day to improve the world and that take little time to accomplish. One simple thing is in learning to smile more often. It's amazing what a simple smile can do in the course of a day. You can also look for opportunities to offer praise and thanks. Again, the simple act of genuinely thanking or praising someone for a job well done can do wonders. Try taking a moment to praise someone you have never seen before for doing something good. Instead of just pointing out faults, take the same amount of energy to seek out chances to offer praise. Another simple thing to do is to practice courtesy. Be friendly and kind to others—even to those who do not deserve it. This kind of act requires developing great patience and inner strength. There's a bumper sticker that I see on cars that proclaims "practice random acts of kindness." That seems to me to be a good motto and a worthwhile spiritual practice. You can offer simple gifts to others or stop and help someone in need. Instead of acting in order to receive praise yourself, a more humble way of acting is to give without such expectations. Giving anonymously or without waiting for thanks emphasizes giving for its own sake.

Exercise 5: Helping Others Through the Physical

Consider your answers to the following questions. I've provided space here for your answers, or you can write them in your journal or some other study guide.

1. What goals do you have for helping others in the physical realm through:

   Helping others grow?

   _____

   _____

   _____

   Simple practices for growth?

   _____

   _____

   _____

Practices for Helping Others: Air

The body is not the only thing that needs growth and development. This is true for ourselves as well as others. We can encourage the mental growth of others primarily by offering to teach. We can teach spiritual concepts to those who seek us out, but we can also teach other basic concepts. Volunteering to help someone read can make a tremendous difference in someone's life. We depend so much on reading. Without reading, people have a difficult time doing almost anything else: filling out tax forms, applying for licenses, getting any education. You obviously have the talent to read, and it is a talent you can share with others. You can also consider helping out in classrooms or other learning situations. Along with the skill to read, people need books that will help them learn and grow. You can offer to help people get books by supporting a local library or offering books to others who have few. What people learn makes a big difference with regard to how they view the world. If a person's reading is limited to only a few subjects and viewpoints, that person will have little knowledge and wisdom with which to engage the world. Insist on the freedom that we have to read all that interests us, and help others to pursue that goal by helping them to learn to read and access the world's great thoughts available through books.

Another way to promote mental growth is to respect the values and opinions of other people even if they are different than your own. So long as the intent to harm is not evident, all value systems have a place and meaning for someone or they would not exist. Religions and philosophies are not just created out of great ideas; they are rooted in the cultural and social context of the creator. If those contexts are different than your own, then it stands to reason that your philosophies will be different than theirs and you may have a difficult time understanding viewpoints different from your own. If you respect the thoughts of others, you will not engage in ridiculing others for their beliefs. This allows people the room to express and explore ideas on their own. Open-minded debate and honest questions can help you to refine your concepts, but insults and disparaging remarks help no one. Doing so is a form of emotional abuse. We often think about abuse only in terms of the physical. Hitting someone is obviously abusive, but so is denying the value of someone's opinion. Abuse can be mental, emotional, or spiritual just as it can be physical. Promoting others mentally means helping others to learn new things and allowing them to form and express their own opinions.

Exercise 6: Helping Others Through the Mental

Consider your answers to the following questions. I've provided space here for your answers, or you can write them in your journal or some other study guide.

1. What goals do you have for helping others in the mental realm through:

    Reading books?

    _____

    _____

    _____

    Respecting and valuing the opinions of others?

    _____

    _____

    _____

Practices for Helping Others: Fire

To help others, you do need to believe in the basic goodness of all people. You know that not all people act in good and just ways. You know that there are a few who are incapable of understanding right from wrong, but that should not stop you from recognizing that all beings begin life with the same spark of Spirit. Knowing this, you can look for ways to love and care for others while also being mindful of the need to protect yourself and our own loved ones from those who seek to cause harm. One way to be more open to others is through hospitality. When it is safe and possible to do so, welcome others to your home, clubs, and spiritual gatherings. Fight the desire to be cold and unfriendly to strangers you meet. You may be thinking that no one has ever done these things for you, so why should you do them for others? The answer comes from the Pagan understanding of energy sent and returned. If you never send out that energy of hospitality into the world, it can never be returned. Rather than waiting for it to happen to you, be the initiator—send that energy forth. Think of it as putting money in the bank: you cannot collect any interest until you first put a sizable amount into your account.

Another way to embrace others is to develop empathy. Empathy is the ability to relate to the feelings of others. Empathy is different than sympathy, where you feel sorry for someone else. It is possible to understand the pains experienced by others without having pity for them as well. In order to have empathy, one must have experienced pain and grief in one's own life. This is the positive side of having had experienced those pains in your own life. We have all had those times when we have cried out, "Why me? Why must I suffer so?" One answer to these questions is that, through the suffering you experienced, you will be better able to help someone else. Through empathy you can understand and comfort others. You come to understand that suffering is part of the condition of life for all beings. The challenge to being empathetic is that some may consider those who are compassionate as "soft" people. There is a social pressure in America, presently, to be hard and tough. I call it the *cowboy mentality*. Certainly there are times when we need to buckle down, get serious, and work hard for what we do, but by not also being compassionate and caring we take the risk of living an unbalanced life, we risk not receiving the compassion and care that we all need, and we create a cold and impassionate world.

Indeed, it is much harder and more challenging to be a compassionate person. The truly brave and strong fight against the urge to conform to simplistic and heartless attitudes. One way to resist that pressure is to not associate with those that espouse those beliefs. It is worth your time and energy to seek out a lifestyle and values that are positive. Find those who can serve as role models or companions in your journey to live the Pagan life. Many times, the people you are with will strongly influence who you are.

Another way to promote the growth of others through the heart is to learn to respect people just for who they are. In a caring family setting, members of the family love and respect each other even though they may quarrel or disagree. They feel a bond for each other that goes deep beyond superficial troubles. You may have heard stories of families who have had troubled children grow up and get in all sorts of trouble with the law or with their teachers. No matter what a troubled child did, that family worked to help that child through the difficulties and challenges. That is a deep and spiritual love. We can learn to develop that kind of love on a more global scale through the simple act of learning to respect others. To respect someone is to value someone regardless of your differences with that person. Respect requires an understanding of the inherent equality of the essence of all beings. Our Pagan theology helps us to recognize this simple but profound truth. We know there is no such thing as "the chosen people." There is no distinction between those who are "saved" and those who are not. Color, sex, place of birth, country, economic status, education, and religion—these are just some of the many things people use to try and set themselves apart from others in order to claim that one group is more deserving than another of the gifts of life. These are all false lines drawn in the sand. Just as the ocean's waves on the beach keep the sand smooth and even, the waves of Spirit that come through in the cycles of life touch all of life evenly.

They say that the fastest way to a person's heart is through his or her stomach. There is certainly a lot of truth in that. Helping to feed others is an act of aiding the physical, but it also a way of aiding the heart. Many of people's greatest childhood memories revolve around events centered on food. Most holidays, and even many Pagan events, center around the act of eating. For this reason, I have put the act of helping to feed others in this section on helping others through the element of Fire and the heart. The epidemic of world hunger is pervasive, and the fact that a rich country such as the United States has so many people who go hungry every day is, to me, shameful. We can do small things to try to help, however. You can offer your money and time to support local food banks and soup kitchens. If you have never helped feed the hungry because it seems that it might be a frightening thing, I can tell you from past experience that it can be a very enlightening and joyful event for you. Unlike a house or clothing that can be used for many years, the need for food is a daily and ongoing requirement for life. Some religions require their practitioners to fast for an extended period of time. One purpose for this act is to understand the importance of the simple gifts we are given and to understand the suffering that others experience when basic needs are not fulfilled. If you have never gone hungry, try fasting for a day or two and you will understand what some people must endure every day of their lives.

Exercise 7: Helping Others Through the Emotional

Consider your answers to the following questions. I've provided space here for your answers, or you can write them in your journal or some other study guide.

1. What goals do you have for helping others in the emotional realm through:

Embracing others?

_____

_____

_____

Respecting others?

_____

_____

_____

Feeding others?

_____

_____

_____

Practices for Helping Others: Water

It is through our own soul that we are closest to Spirit. This is true for all. By promoting the soul of others, we promote our own soul and come closer to experiencing the single source of energy that is the essence of all life. Promoting the soul requires a combined effort of all the other elements we have discussed so far. Encouraging physical, mental, and emotional growth develops the soul's capacity to be in the world and to let the beauty of Spirit emerge. Aiding others physically, mentally, and emotionally brings us all closer together and encourages dialogue, interaction, and peace. We can promote the growth of the soul through healing. Healing is another thing that is more than physical. You can work to heal the body, but you can also work to heal the mind and the heart. Doing so allows the soul to grow. You do not necessarily have to be a trained doctor to heal. Sometimes just giving a hand to those who are in need, taking a few moments to listen deeply to someone who is hurting, or letting someone know that there is actually another person that cares in this world can go a long way to healing a pained soul.

Sometimes, the best gift we can give to others is ourselves. You can offer a lot by simply being present with someone. I don't mean just appearing somewhere and standing idly by. What I mean is that you can offer your energies to others by giving them your full attention and care. One of the best ways to do this is to be fully present with others when you are listening to them. Some people need only to have someone listen with an open mind and an open heart. Taking the time to truly listen to someone is, in itself, a very spiritual act. Most people do not really listen to others when they speak. In order to listen deeply to someone else, you have to truly care about what he or she has to say and you must feel that what he or she has to say is important. Some people, especially those who may be in hurt, just need someone to listen to them and care about what they have to say. You do not have to always offer solutions—someone else may need to do that for them—but you can offer them a chance to be heard. Through your connection to Spirit, you can offer positive energies and offer spiritual healing by just paying attention.

Another way to help aid others spiritually is through our own spiritual practices. Pagans do not believe in trying to force our religion on others, but this does not have to mean that we hide our spiritual practice, either. There are those in the world who are searching for a religious practice that touches their hearts and souls. If you feel comfortable doing so, let others know what you believe, that you are proud to be Pagan, and that it is a spirituality that deepens your connection to yourself, to others, and to the Spirit of the universe. They will see through your sense of peace and joy in life that your religion is meaningful, and they will want to know more. Be willing to know and share the answers to those questions that people ask you. I know there is still a lot of ignorance and fear about our spiritual practice, but I believe that, in time, this will change. If sharing your spiritual views would risk danger to you or your loved ones then, by all means, remain silent, but keeping the great joy of Paganism a secret is no longer a necessity. The more we let our religion grow, the less we need to fear about the ignorance of others concerning our faith. When it seems appropriate, invite those who ask about Pagan rituals to your ceremonies. If someone is just starting out on the Pagan path, be willing to mentor him or her. Help others obtain the tools and materials they need to begin their study and practice. Be willing to plant some spiritual seeds in the ground and then, when a sprout appears, care for it until it grows and blossoms.

Spiritual growth is both a personal activity and a community activity. Helping others through the soul can be done through community activism where you put your Pagan values into practice. You can work by yourself or with other groups to help put forth and defend issues that are important to you and your spiritual principles. Deciding to help others through a community project or organization is a worthwhile spiritual goal, but careful planning is needed to be effective. You must first decide which causes are most important to you, and then figure out how much time, money, and energy you can actually offer before looking for an opportunity to help. Having done this, you can then search for an organization that you feel best aids the causes that are important to you. Of course, you can always consider designing your own project or event to help out. This involves more time and energy, but it is a way to ensure that energy is going exactly where you wish it to go.

To turn community activism from a chore into a spiritual practice, you can observe three steps:

1. Determine a worthwhile act of service or issue that needs a particular focus.

2. Release all desires from it.

3. Learn from the experience.

A worthwhile project is, again, one that has meaning to you. It should also be an act that is easy enough for you to accomplish while still being effective enough to make a positive impact regardless of how small that impact may be. It needs to be an action in which you can truly and effectively commit some of your time and energy. Once you have chosen a focus, then you need to let go of any external desires that can be attached to it. Release the natural desire to be thanked, praised, or recognized. If any of these things happen, great. But they are not the goal of your activity. The desire to do community activism is to help and to know that you have played a small part in making a difference in the world and in the lives of other beings. Then, after you have completed the project, look back over it and observe what you have learned. It can be hard to see the benefits of an act when you are in the middle of it. Sometimes it is best to wait until you are through and can take a look from the distance. Learn from one activity and then place that knowledge into the planning and execution of your next project.

Exercise 8: Helping Others Through the Spiritual

Consider your answers to the following questions. I've provided space here for your answers, or you can write them in your journal or some other study guide.

1. What goals do you have for helping others in the spiritual realm through:

   Healing others?

   _____

   _____

   _____

   Listening and being present?

   _____

   _____

   _____

Spreading Pagan ideals?

_____

_____

_____

Community activism?

_____

_____

_____

Practices for Helping Others: Seeking Balance

When developing parts of the self, we can forget that we also need to help others. Conversely, when helping others, we can forget to take care of ourselves. Again, balance must be sought in order to maintain health and happiness. We cannot help others if we run our own selves into the ground. Always balance work with rest, and help with reflection.

Practices for Honoring Gaia and Spirit

> ### General goals for honoring Gaia and Spirit:
>
> ▷ Honor Gaia.
>
> ▷ Honor Spirit.

Practices for Gaia and Spirit: Gaia

Part of our spiritual practice includes the belief that Gaia is a living being. We all inhabit the home of Mother Earth, but, as can children that run rampant inside a house, we have come to the realization that we are capable of destroying our own home. We do not believe that this world was given to us as a Christmas present for us to use up and manipulate as we wish. With each step and breath upon the face of Gaia we help to influence Her destiny. Part of our spiritual practice, then, needs to include ways in which we can heal, restore, and honor Gaia. One of the most profound and simple ways is simply to be with Gaia as much as possible. You can take walks in nature or go camping and hiking. You can visit local parks and open spaces. You can go canoeing, or go out on a rowboat or sailboat. You can go biking, or just sit outside the house and watch the birds or the stars. Whatever you do, take some time to simply admire the many wonders of Gaia. From the greatest mountain to the tiniest detail in the design of a leaf, She provides plenty of beauty to admire, smells to enjoy, interesting surfaces to touch, beautiful colors and shapes to behold, and mysteries to ponder.

We can also honor the many cycles of Gaia. By honoring these cycles, we pay our respect to Her and find time to offer our gratitude for having such a beautiful home. As are all things, Gaia is constantly changing and renewing Herself. Each day, the sun opens his arms and welcomes us to his light and warmth. With changes in weather and the seasons, the sun appears to us differently throughout the year and the days. We can honor the sun and welcome the chance for another day to be whole and alive. The moon is also always changing. Each night she appears to us with a different face. She travels the night sky and sparks our imaginations. You can honor her when her light is full and when she appears to be completely dark. At the dark moon, you get your best chance to observe the beauty of the millions of stars that have sent their light our way. The shapes created by their positions in the sky have been thought to be symbolic messages from the gods for many thousands of years. There are also special times in your life when you can stop and offer praise and gratitude. These are the personal and social milestones that we all experience as we live and grow. (We will explore these opportunities in more detail in Chapter 3.)

Gaia is a single planet among billions and, though it seems huge to us, it is really very small. Gaia is a grand mother to us but, as with any mother, Her resources are limited. Like a cancer, the human population continues to populate the planet and use up these precious resources. If growth continues unchecked, we will destroy our Mother and our home. You can help to heal and maintain our planet through simple ecology practices, including picking up trash, recycling, and doing basic conservation. Organizing groups to pick up trash is a great way to be in nature and help keep our lands green at the same time. Many neighborhoods now regularly recycle goods, but sometimes not everything is recycled. We need to keep up efforts to maintain recycling of many different products at home and at work. We need to encourage the use of more recyclable and biodegradable materials. Besides recycling, we also need to conserve what we can. Simple conservation mostly involves just being aware of how much something is used.

Doing things such as recycling, creating biodegradable materials, and conservation is one side of the economic spectrum related to simple ecology. The other side is to be observant of the products we buy. In a capitalistic society, every product we buy is a political action. That is because our economy is based on competition between companies that produce the products we buy. Every time you buy a product, you make a choice and a statement about the kinds of products you want to see created and sold. If you demand Gaia-friendly products and can convince others to do the same, producers will hear the sound of your money and work to fill the demand. This will only happen, of course, if there are enough people demanding those types of products. But we have to begin somewhere and not wait for everyone else to join us in order to make an impact. It does no good to blame the companies; they make what they think will sell. The responsibility comes down to all of us. Shop wisely and know what impact your buying power has on the fate of our mother Gaia.

Yet another type of ecology is called *deep ecology*. Arnie Naess, a Norwegian philosopher, coined this term in 1972. He proclaimed that it is a scientific truth that all living systems on this planet are connected and related, and that believing that humankind is the height and center of these systems is simply not true. We are not the masters of this planet. We are one of the many interconnected systems that depend on each other for survival. Naess went on to say that we need to learn to identify ourselves with these living systems instead of with ourselves. In this way, we see ourselves as part of a large, living planetary family and not just small units of humans fighting against nature to survive. This is a way of thinking and being that can affect our whole lives. Through deep ecological thinking, we think differently about ourselves, our relationships to others, and our relationship to all of life on this planet.

Honoring Gaia can also happen by accepting and being thankful for the many blessings She bestows on us every day. Every day, you take in food from Her bounty, you breathe the air that She holds within Her arms through the atmosphere, you lie down upon Her as you sleep for the night, and you wear clothes made from Her gifts (or we should). Every day on this planet there are beautiful sights, sounds, smells, and tastes to behold that are gifts freely given to all from this planet. Take some time to honor these gifts by recognizing and enjoying them and then thanking Gaia and Spirit for being given the chance to experience them.

Exercise 9: Honoring Gaia

Consider your answers to the following questions. I've provided space here for your answers, or you can write them in your journal or some other study guide.

1. What goals do you have for honoring Gaia through:

Being in nature?

_____

_____

_____

_____

Simple ecology?

_____

_____

_____

_____

Deep ecology?

_____

_____

_____

_____

The many blessings of Gaia?

_____

_____

_____

_____

Practices for Gaia and Spirit: Spirit

Though all of the activities I have discussed so far can be classified as spiritual in nature, sometimes it is important to recognize and honor the goal of the spiritual pursuit that is Spirit itself. In practices for Spirit, we take time to honor the source of the energies of Expression, Envelopment, and Balance that makes it possible to enjoy life and love others. We can also learn to tap into this energy in order to bless others.

We have each been given gifts from Spirit. You have life. You have a mother Gaia, who cradles you. You might be blessed with a loving family and friends. You may have found a mentor or a spiritual community with whom you can learn and share. You may have developed a relationship with the divine or a loving deity. These are all relationships to those things that nurture and sustain you. Honor those gifts you have been given as often as you can. Be thankful for what you may have regardless of how little it may seem. As you work to develop other relationships, be sure to honor and be thankful for them as well. Recognizing this fact, we can take time to honor Spirit through whatever deity or universal concept with which we are most comfortable. You are more than a single person, a single ego. You are connected to a greater wholeness. You can be thankful for what you have and ask for strength and energy to seek what you truly need.

Honoring Spirit can be as simple as offering a few brief thoughts or words of thanks to the universe for the gifts you have been given, or as complex as doing a long ritual. Honoring Spirit begins by recognizing those gifts. The simple things that we often take for granted on a daily basis are some of those regular gifts. For those with a stable life, many of these simple things are considered daily expectations. Those who are not so fortunate as to have these things can be keenly aware of how important they are. If you become more aware of these gifts, you can be reminded of their importance and of the basic needs that all living things require.

Our relationships include all those we would call friends—both human and non-human. These are beings to whom you offer love and support, and to whom you look to for the same. Our families are those people who, hopefully, provide a sense of home, protection, and belonging. Families should be based upon love and respect, and should not be defined by the types of people in the family but by the relationships of the family members. Gay couples provide just as much family structure, support, and love as do many straight couples. The gender, race, number, or even religion of a family is not what determines the level of love and compassion that maintains it. As with all good relationships, the strength of a family depends upon the commitment made by all the members to lovingly support the growth, expression, and interrelationship of all of its members. Mentors and teachers or members of a spiritual community are those who offer special wisdom in our search for personal or spiritual growth. These relationships can offer the same benefits of a family structure except, of course, that members are not necessarily born into the group. People in a spiritual community choose each other because they desire to associate with those who have similar beliefs. A strong spiritual community should also make a commitment to its members to support spiritual growth, expression, and relationship.

Though there are those who do not enjoy work, one can still be grateful for the opportunity to have employment and to make a difference, however small, on the job. For those who do have a job they enjoy, the reason for being thankful is even greater. We can also be thankful for having a home and a place to be warm, dry, and safe. For those who are so fortunate, consider what it would be like to not have a home. Consider what it would be like to live on the street. You develop compassion for those who do not have homes by considering these thoughts, and you develop an appreciation for your own gifts. Each meal is also a gift. Every day, people work to make it possible for us to eat. Gaia provides us with raw food materials, and we and others combine these elements into meals. You must eat to remain connected to Gaia, and so you can take an opportunity to thank Her for continuing to provide and offer you sustenance. You can also be thankful for the rising of the sun in the morning, giving us yet another day to live and fulfill our potential as beings of Spirit. We can be thankful for the coming of the evening, when we can relax and take stock of what we have done through the day. Lastly, we can be thankful for the peaceful rest of sleep that lets our minds fly to the heights of imagination and settle into the quiet of the darkness.

For each of these gifts we can take a brief moment to offer thanks to Gaia, our deities, or to Spirit. To whom we offer these prayers of gratitude is less important than the frame of mind and the level of sincerity with which we offer them. You can offer thanks through ornate and beautiful rituals or through a few heartfelt words. You can present your expressions outwardly or inwardly. It depends on which method is most comfortable to you. For example, before eating a meal you could offer a prayer of thanks by conducting a ritual of thanksgiving. A simpler method would be to audibly speak a prayer of thanks. An even more simple method would be to silently contemplate a prayer to yourself or consider the meaning of this gift of food. If being in a group of people who would not understand your actions means that you prefer an even less conspicuous act of silent prayer, you could internally speak a prayer as you bring your first drink to your lips—a kind of spiritual toast to the universe. You can offer a blessing for anything and do it with as much bravado or inconspicuousness as you feel is right.

Besides accepting the blessings we receive, there are ways in which we can also offer thanks to others and to Spirit. The various cycles of the universe also offer us opportunities to give thanks and celebrate life. There are monthly cycles of the moon. Full moons and dark moons as well as the subdivision of those changes we call *weeks* all present special chances to celebrate. The solar cycle of the year and its seasons, combined with moon patterns, provide times for special occasions and events. In these events, you can take time to be thankful for the life-giving changes that take place. We can also be thankful for the many blessings and changes that happen throughout our lives. Our bodies change and grow. We develop love relationships and families. There are always special moments of joy that can be celebrated alone or with others. Each of these is an opportunity to thank the universe.

In thanking the universe for offering the gifts of life to us, we are accepting the blessings bestowed upon us. We are not blessed because we are special, but because we are all part of the same great spiritual dance of the cosmos. In gratitude, we thank Spirit for all we have but we also recognize that Spirit is within us—that we are Spirit as well. Because of this fact, we can also bless others by bringing forth energy ourselves. Through practices such as meditation and ritual, we can learn to access the universal energy and work to direct this energy at will. This is the essence of magick. We can begin with our own selves by bringing energy into our own bodies and lives. One simple method is to visualize energy from the earth being drawn up through the body. This energy can be experienced as warmth or envisioned as a light. Each person relates to it differently. Feel this essence filling and enriching you. Feel the strength of the energy of Expression and the joy of the energy of Envelopment within you. Pay careful attention to the parts of your body that seem to need more energy and work with those areas. Just as a rechargeable battery can, you can recharge each day and then spread this energy through your blessings. Learn to take time to draw Earth energy and cosmic energy into your body so that you can use this energy to help yourself and others. Also learn to ground this energy by returning it back to Gaia and the universe when it is not needed.

You can offer your blessings to others through prayers or kind words, or you can direct it through simple visualizations or feelings. This sharing can be done to all beings: pets, plants, animals, trees, or any part of Earth. Blessings can be offered to any person, whether close friend or stranger on the street. You can offer blessings through your conversations. Through thoughtful expressions and words of praise, you can offer energy to another person. Many magickal workings include the use of chants and songs because words are powerful ways of expressing intent and directing energy. If you consider all words that you speak as emitting energy and intent from deep within, you will know that all of your words are significant and that all of your expressions are magickal. It is important, however, to remember that these blessings come not *from* you but *through* you. You are the conduit through which Spirit speaks and touches others.

Through these blessings, we can act as agents of Spirit and desire for all beings need the same things. We can encourage all beings to grow and live to their full potential. We can encourage all beings to experience life to its fullest, and we can encourage love, compassion, and understanding.

Exercise 10: Honoring Spirit

Consider your answers to the following questions. I've provided space here for your answers, or you can write them in your journal or some other study guide.

1. What goals do you have for honoring Spirit through:

    Accepting blessings of Spirit?

    _____

    _____

    _____

    _____

    _____

    Offering blessings of Spirit?

    _____

    _____

    _____

    _____

    _____

Practices for Gaia and Spirit: Seeking Balance

A danger with any spiritual practice is the possibility of taking things too seriously. All the things we have discussed so far are important to the practicing Pagan, but so is finding and living the joy of life. Any spiritual pursuit needs to be filled with both serious work and fun. To seek Balance while accepting and offering blessings to Gaia and Spirit is to find time to also enjoy those blessings. If you can accept the gifts you have been given with gratitude and, at the same time, be mindful of the joy and magick that each can bring to your life, you will truly be living a Pagan life. There is great joy to be found in each of our relationships if those relationships are equally nurturing and supportive. If your work is meaningful, you can find joy in it. If your home life is full of mutual compassion, you can find great joy in that as well. You can take time to truly enjoy eating meals, rising in the morning, and preparing for bed at night. Without a healthy helping of joy mixed into our recipe for practice, we will simply be adding more chores to our list of things to get done.

You can also seek joy and live the Pagan life by finding ways to bring magick into life. Magick is an act of willful transformation, and there are many things that you could help transform for the better. You can begin with your own life, and that is the focus of this book. By developing a Pagan spiritual practice that includes honoring the sacred cycles and gifts of Spirit and, consequently, finding joy in life through these practices, you will begin to willfully and with intent transform yourself into a true, living Pagan. With this joy and the power of the magick you will discover in this transformation, you will then begin to transform others and spread your magick wherever you go.

Practices for Honoring Yourself and Others

> ### General goals for honoring Gaia and Spirit:
> ▷ Honor yourself and your life events.
>
> ▷ Honor others and their life events.

Earlier in this chapter, we looked at setting spiritual goals for the development of the self. In this section, we will look at how you can come to honor yourself and others. I invite you to learn to celebrate yourself and the continually changing, blossoming, and awakening person that you are and will become. I also invite you to be active in helping others to celebrate their lives as well, for this is how we create a community of supportive and caring people. To celebrate yourself and the lives of others is to create pride. Some confuse pride with arrogance. They are two different things entirely. Pride is a strong and positive attribute through which you display a strength, courage, and surety of who you are. When people decide that their sense of inner strength gives them license to consider themselves greater or more deserving than another, that is arrogance. If you are proud of yourself, who you are, and what you believe, but also recognize that other people deserve the chance to be proud of themselves because you are all equal in the universe, then you should feel good about your well-placed sense of pride. As with the other practices we have been observing, it is important to celebrate all the parts of your self and to do so in balance.

Practices for Honoring Yourself and Others: Honoring Yourself

Through the element of Earth you can learn to honor your body and learn to take spiritual retreats. Unfortunately, we live in a society where honoring the body is not considered a positive thing—unless, of course, you have the most unlikely figure of some supermodel. You are asked on a daily basis to compare your body to some impossible standard of beauty designed by advertisers. The aim of every marketing campaign is to try and convince you that your life is incomplete and that your body is inadequate. Without convincing you of this idea, you would not feel a need to purchase those many products that are designed to satisfy your needs and fix your shortcomings. This type of message not only creates false images, but it can also be extremely damaging to the health and psyche of many people. Some people spend a great deal of their lives and money trying to be something they are not so that they can fit into a preconditioned mold. You cannot fit a square peg in a round hole no matter how hard you try, and I will never look like Tom Cruise no matter what I buy—nor would I ever want to. Your body and my body are special and unique. You can strive to be healthy and fit, and you can work to avoid adding excess weight that may be detrimental to your health, but you cannot make your body into something it is not. Come to learn about your unique body: its gifts, its faults, its own inner and outer beauty. Celebrate who you are, because it is who you are and because you are like no one else that has ever appeared or will ever again. Celebrate your uniqueness and the beauty of your individual shape, color, and form.

Another way to honor your body is to give it a vacation. Specifically, plan to take a spiritual retreat at least once a year. A retreat can be as long as one day, a weekend, or even longer. A spiritual vacation gives you a chance to more fully connect with your deities, Gaia, and Spirit. To take a spiritual retreat, take some time to design your schedule so that you will practice those things that help you make that deeper connection. I suggest that you actually draw up a plan for yourself so that you will not fall into boredom or feel at a loss for what you should do during your retreat. Be flexible with the plan, however. Spirit may move you in different ways, and you should honor and respect that. If going off to a retreat all by yourself does not appeal to you, then look for a Pagan retreat in your area. There are often groups who offer retreat weekends and activities. There are also retreat centers throughout the country. Some are Pagan, most are not, but some will accept people of different faiths. Of course, if you have the energy and drive, you could design a retreat yourself and invite others to come join you. There are many people from many different religious traditions who will tell you that a weeklong spiritual retreat helps them feel refreshed and spiritually recharged enough for a whole year.

As you learn to honor your body, you can also learn to honor your thoughts through the element of Air. What has been said about the body can also be true for the mind. Again, we are given messages that we should be unsure of ourselves. That way, others (the "experts" and "authorities") can come to tell you how you should think. I deal with this in the art world all the time. People are always telling me that they know nothing about music or art, implying that they could not possibly form an opinion about a work. You do not need to know anything to determine if an artistic creation touches your soul. Of course, it helps to have some knowledge and experience with art in order to widen your exposure and understanding of it, but no amount of knowledge is needed to know whether or not you are moved by someone's art. Respect the fact that you will never be able to know all things, that others may know things you do not, and that your opinion is as valuable as anyone else's view. Beyond that, honor your own thoughts and ever-evolving feelings about things.

Learn to practice positive self-speech. Too many times our minds are filled with negative thoughts—especially about ourselves. This is true for those who were raised in negative environments. Your mind is a powerful instrument and is the strongest magickal tool you will ever posses. With it, you can learn to visualize a more magickal and Pagan-centered life. You can practice positive self-speech and create positive visualizations in your mind to help direct your self-image, attitude, and reactions you want to have as a practicing Pagan in the world.

Through the element of Fire you can learn to honor the energy you put forth in the world through your works. If you know within your heart that you have worked to do the very best in everything that you do, then you can take pride in your work even if the result does not always turn out the way you want. Regardless of what others say, it is you who must make the final determination about what you do in this world. You can get opinions and learn how to do things better, but the final judgment must always remain your own. Be honest with yourself about what you do. Judge yourself fairly and learn from your mistakes, but, most of all, value your own thoughts.

Through Water you can come to value your own spirituality. In a pluralistic society it can become easy to feel isolated. This is even more so when your spiritual values are considered to be in the minority. There will always be pressure to try to conform to the dominant philosophy or theology, but, as long as you live in a free society, you can be proud of your own way of relating to the universe. A Pagan spiritual community is a good way to find others who have similar thoughts and feelings. If you are feeling a little outnumbered in terms of your spiritual view of life, consider joining or starting a Pagan spiritual community. Honoring your spiritual self also means honoring the call that Spirit makes to you. By listening deeply and learning to connect to the wisdom of the universe, you can learn to hear to what you are called. A spiritual call is usually related to joining the ministry, but it does not always need to be. You can feel a call to do most anything—usually something positive and growing for you and the world. Some feel called to teach, some are called to become artists, and others are called to work in the health fields. You have a unique body, a unique mind, and a unique set of viewpoints. You also have a unique purpose in the world. If you listen carefully and pay attention to the signs the universe gives you, you may be able to discover your calling.

Exercise 11: Honoring Yourself

Consider your answers to the following questions. I've provided space here for your answers, or you can write them in your journal or some other study guide.

1. What goals do you have for honoring yourself through Earth by: Honoring your body?

_____

_____

_____

Spiritual retreats?

_____

_____

_____

_____

2. What goals do you have for honoring yourself through Air by:
    Honoring your thoughts?

    _____

    _____

    _____

    _____

    Positive self-speech?

    _____

    _____

    _____

    _____

    Positive visualizations?

    _____

    _____

    _____

    _____

3. What goals do you have for honoring yourself through Fire by:
    Honoring your good works?

    _____

    _____

    _____

    _____

4. What goals do you have for honoring yourself through Water by:
    Honoring your theology?

    _____

    _____

    _____

    Being in spiritual community?

    _____

    _____

    _____

    Finding your call?

    _____

    _____

    _____

Practices for Honoring Yourself and Others: Honoring Others

The other side of the coin of honoring yourself is to also honor others. As you honor the natural beauty and form of your body through the element of Earth, you can also honor the form and shape of others and appreciate their natural beauty. Through Air, you can learn to honor the thoughts and opinions of others. With the element of Fire, you can develop the ability to honor the work of people around you. And with Water, you can honor the spirituality and call of those who come to share those things with you.

Exercise 12: Honoring Others

Consider your answers to the following questions. I've provided space here for your answers, or you can write them in your journal or some other study guide.

1. What goals do you have for honoring others through Earth by: Honoring the bodies of others?

    _____

    _____

    _____

    _____

2. What goals do you have for honoring others through Air by: Honoring the thoughts of others?

    _____

    _____

    _____

    _____

3. What goals do you have for honoring others through Fire by: Honoring the works of others?

    _____

    _____

    _____

    _____

4. What goals do you have for honoring others through Water by: Honoring the spirituality of others?

_____

_____

_____

_____

A Summary of Goals

We have reviewed a variety of practices that can be done to develop and improve the self, help others, honor Gaia and Spirit, and honor yourself and others. It is time now to put together all these goals that you have chosen and add them to your spiritual practice and Pagan life. Following this section are sample charts to show you how to get started. There is a separate chart for each of the four categories we have discussed in this chapter: developing the self, helping others, honoring Gaia and Spirit, and honoring yourself and others. In the left-hand column under "Goal" are the general goals as mentioned in this text. The column marked "Activity" includes one of the specific activities related to the general goal listed in the first column. In the next four columns, the elements are listed by their first letters: Earth (E), Air (A), Fire (F), and Water (W). A check has been placed in the column of the element to which the activity is connected. The next two columns are used to check whether the activity may be considered fun or challenging (work). The final column marks how frequent (marked "Freq.") the activity should take place: *D* is for daily activities, *M* for monthly, *Y* for yearly, and *I* for activities that come at irregular times.

Practices for Developing the Self

Goal	Activity	E	A	F	W	Work	Fun	Freq.
Physical Expression	Going for walks	x					x	D
Physical Envelopment	Getting a massage	x					x	M
Mental Expression	Being honest with others		x			x		D
Mental Expression	Writing a journal		x			x		W
Mental Envelopment	Studying spiritual and other topics of interest		x			x		W
Emotional Expression	Expressing feelings through creativity			x			x	M
Emotional Envelopment	Being open to others' feelings			x			x	D
Emotional Envelopment	Reminding others that you care for them			x		x		M
Soulful Expression	Seeking pleasure and joy				x		x	D
Soulful Envelopment	Meditating				x	x		D
Soulful Envelopment	Seeking inspiration from dreams				x	x		D
DEVELOPING THE SELF TOTALS		2	3	3	3	6	5	

Practices for Helping Others

GOAL	ACTIVITY	E	A	F	W	WORK	FUN	FREQ.
Physical Aid	Donating money to help organizations	x				x		M
Physical Aid	Working in soup kitchens	x					x	Y
Mental Aid	Valuing the thoughts and opinions of others		x			x		D
Mental Aid	Volunteering to teach		x				x	M
Emotional Aid	Being hospitable when possible			x		x		I
Emotional Aid	Encouraging others to honor and value their feelings			x		x		D
Soulful Aid	Respecting the religion of others				x	x		D
Soulful Aid	Providing healing when possible				x		x	I
	HELPING OTHERS TOTALS	2	2	2	2	5	3	

Practices for Gaia and Spirit

In this chart, the columns for the four elements have been left off, because Mother Gaia (G) contains the four elements, and Spirit (S) is the essence of those elements.

Goal	Activity	G	S	Work	Fun	Freq.
Honoring Spirit	Esbat ritual		x		x	M
Honoring Spirit	Astor ritual		x		x	M
Honoring Spirit	Sabbat ritual		x		x	Y
Honoring Spirit	Practicing honest communication		x	x		D
Honoring Spirit	Practicing ethics		x	x		D
Honoring Gaia	Saying blessings before meals	x		x		D
Honoring Gaia	Practicing simple ecology	x		x		W
Honoring Gaia	Practicing deep ecology	x			x	W
Honoring Gaia	Spending time in nature	x			x	W
Honoring Gaia	Taking stock of the day's blessings	x	x		x	D
	Gaia and Spirit Totals	5	6	4	6	

Practices for Honoring Yourself and Others

Goal	Activity	E	A	F	W	Work	Fun	Freq.
Honoring yourself and others	Honoring your body	x				x		W
Honoring yourself and others	Taking spiritual breaks and vacations	x						DMY
Honoring yourself and others	Practicing positive self-speech		x			x		D
Honoring yourself and others	Practicing positive visualizations for the day		x			x		D
Honoring yourself and others	Practicing with a spiritual community			x			x	W
Honoring yourself and others	Celebrating life events				x		x	Y
Honoring yourself and others	Celebrating life events of others				x		x	Y
Honoring Yourself and Others Totals		2	2	1	2	3	3	
Totals for All Practices		6	7	6	7	17	18	

Your Own Charts

Now that you have an idea of how to set up your personal Pagan spiritual goals through the use of these charts, you can set up your own charts. When you are done, review the entire chart and see if the number of goals is balanced between the elements and whether or not the work activities are balanced with fun activities. If not, consider revising the chart until it becomes more balanced. When complete, the chart may appear a bit daunting, but keep in mind that you do not need to incorporate all these goals at once. It may actually take you years to create the kind of Pagan life you desire. We will take a look at how to incorporate these goals over time in the next chapter. What you will be creating is an ultimate set of goals for yourself.

3

The Cycles and Their Significance

Introduction

In Chapter 2, I discussed the many different natural cycles that affect our lives: the cycles of Gaia, the moon, and the sun, and our own life cycles. Each of these creates particular events, such as the day, the week, the phases of the moon, the month, the year, and the cycles of birth and death. Some cycles create regular events that affect us and that have the same meaning for all. For example, all beings on Earth experience the rising of the sun as the beginning of a day (at least in terms of light). For many, the appearance of the sun's light means that it is time to rise from sleep and begin the day's activities. Even those for whom this might not be true, the sunrise still marks the beginning of a new day. Each cyclic event can have a common meaning, but it can also be attributed a special meaning. For some, the appearance of a full moon might signify nothing more than a beautiful night. For others, a full moon represents magick and mystery, or it can be a symbol of the feminine energy of deity. These types of meanings are more personal. In this chapter, we will look at all these cycles and find a variety of meanings that may be attributed to each.

The Cycles of Gaia

Every 24 hours Gaia rotates on Her axis, revealing a portion of Her surface to the light and warmth of the sun. We call this the *cycle of days*. Each year holds a minimum of 365 of these days. As it is with anything that occurs repeatedly on a regular basis, it is easy to begin to feel "caught in a rut." Days can begin to melt into one another in an endless chain of sleep, work, eat, and sleep. Without a spiritual focus, a continuous chain of days can become tedious and meaningless. Use the cycle of the day to remind yourself of your spiritual values, and let the day become a time of regular practice.

In the development of the Pagan spiritual life there will be regular days and there will be days that are considered special. You will eventually develop a standard practice for different parts of the regular day that are consistent. Then there will be days in which you will incorporate special events and practices. In reality, all the cycles discussed in this book will have their effect and will be experienced through the cycle of the day. Special days will be determined by moon phases, the change of seasons, and changes in life.

Regular Days

I believe that there are three important factors to any spiritual practice. A spiritual practice must be:

1. Meaningful to the practitioner.

2. Consistent.

3. Flexible.

The first requirement only makes sense. If a religious practice is not meaningful, then it will have little effect on the one following it. Anyone can go through the ritual procedures of a particular religion, but if it has no inner significance, there will be no meaningful change or connection for that person. The second requirement, that a practice be consistent, is the most difficult part of any practice. Many people start a practice because it may provide some excitement to the day, but quickly drop it when the luster wears off. A spiritual practice can only have a lasting positive effect if it is regularly practiced (hence, the word *practice*). The normal routine of the day provides opportunities for developing a regular practice. Incorporate those things that are meaningful to you into a consistent daily practice and continue with them. Be persistent and practice even when you no longer feel like doing it, because it is often during these times that real changes take place. Just as with lifting weights, if we stopped when it begins to hurt a little, there will be no growth. Use the cycle of the regular day to push through the barrier of boredom. Find meaning in the day and let its consistency provide guidance to your practice.

The third requirement of a spiritual practice, that it be flexible, may seem contradictory to the second. If persistence is necessary, then changing the routine would appear to be detrimental to the practice, and this is true—to a point. If, after following a practice, a breakthrough is made or a sense of spiritual connection is maintained and strengthened, you are on the right path. But if that persistence does nothing but create more stress and disillusion, flexibility is called for. The only way to tell the difference between the desire to break the practice because of boredom and the need to change a practice because that is what would be required to continue growth is to develop the wisdom and deep honesty with yourself to know what you truly need. Sometimes circumstances change and a practice needs also to be changed. For example, if you are used to meditating in the morning and your job schedule changes so that you now have to get up earlier, flexibility allows you to make some adjustments and still find a way to maintain your practice. Another example would be if a special day comes along, such as your birthday or a holiday. On such a day you might want to alter your practice to reflect the meaning of the day or you might even want to curtail your practice for a day to get some much-needed rest and relaxation. Being flexible allows you to do these things and not feel out of alignment with your values. Through the repetition of the regular day, you can create and continue a regular and consistent spiritual practice, but, with the addition of special days created by the different cycles, you can add some flexibility and variety to your overall practice.

Exercise 1: Regular Days

 Consider your answers to the following questions. I've provided space here for your answers, or you can write them in your journal or some other study guide.

1. What to you is the significance of the regular day?

_____

_____

_____

_____

Divisions of the Regular Day

Each day of every year presents you with another opportunity to develop and continue your Pagan spiritual practice. To help learn how to do this, the day can be further divided into four quarters: dawn (midnight to 6 a.m.), morning (from 6 a.m. to noon), afternoon (from noon to 6 p.m.), and dusk (6 p.m. to midnight). In each of these quarters, there are usually certain activities that happen regularly, and we can use each of these as an opportunity to maintain a Pagan spiritual practice. The four quarters of the day can be related to the four phases of the moon or to what is known as the four faces of the Goddess. (Traditionally, there are only three, but I prefer four.) Those four faces are the child, the maiden, the mother, and the crone. Similarly, the four faces of the God would be called the child, the suitor, the father, and the sage.

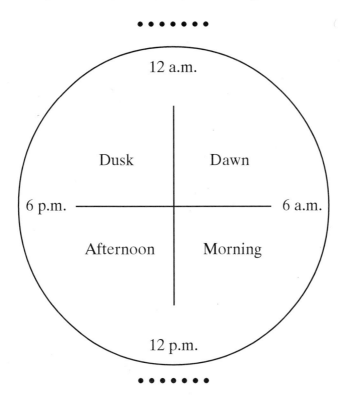

Dawn is the child of the day. As children we like to explore our environments as we learn to define who and what we are. For most people the dawn quarter of the day is used for sleeping. Through our dreams we explore the mysteries of our deep unconscious and the universe. Images of people and things become objects of play for us in the midst of the night. Our minds use sleep to restore our bodies through rest. As we sleep, we hug Gaia and can even assume fetal positions as we recall the warmth and protection of the womb. We are connected directly to Spirit through symbols and through the pure quiet of just being. At dawn we look for the first signs of light and absorb the energy of the new day.

Morning is the maiden of the day. As maidens and suitors in life, we look to develop and strengthen our relationship with other people. We develop interests in groups and in group identity. We look for connections and, specifically, we begin to look for a relationship with someone whom we hope to build a life. In the morning quarter of the day, we prepare ourselves to interact with others. For many it is the time of preparation before work or school. How you wake and the attitudes you define for yourself in the morning will affect the rest of the day. You can choose how you wish to see yourself for that day and then find ways to hold on to that image you have created. At morning we move toward the full light of the midday sun. Our energies are usually on the rise until it is time for lunch.

Afternoon is the mother of the day. In the mother/father phase of life we begin to create a life with love and begin to care for others, either through our own children or with the children of others we know. That same attitude of caring also gets extended to those we know and to the world in general. In the afternoon of the day, we eat a noontime meal, continue our engagements with others, and then prepare to return home. All of this can be done literally or figuratively. Mentally and spiritually, the effect is the same. The afternoon is a time to continue to practice relationships with others. It starts with the waning of the light of the sun, as we begin to feel the same drain of energy. We may get a small boost from lunch, but soon after we will begin to tire until it is time for dinner.

Dusk is the crone of the day. As crones and sages in life, we begin to look back upon our own histories. We become wise from years of experience, and this wisdom is passed on to others. In this stage we begin to cast off the burdens of the work years and learn to enjoy the simplicities of life. This can also be a very spiritual era for people who have the time to pursue spiritual interests and callings. The dusk of the day is when we return home to our families to gather together for dinner and, hopefully, begin to relax for the evening. Dusk can also be a time for spiritual connection and renewal. It is during this time that the light of the sun fades into the darkness of night. As the light retires, so do we prepare to retire for the evening and look to begin the day's cycle again.

Exercise 2: The Divisions of the Day

Consider your answers to the following questions. I've provided space here for your answers, or you can write them in your journal or some other study guide.

1. What significance does each of the following quarters of the day hold for you?

    Dawn.

    _____

    _____

    _____

    _____

Morning.

_____

_____

_____

_____

_____

Afternoon.

_____

_____

_____

_____

_____

Dusk.

_____

_____

_____

_____

_____

Days of Celebration

Some special days have religious or spiritual significance, and some have personal significance. With these days, we take a break from the routine and celebrate something unique. Some days are holy days or holidays that have spiritual significance. For Pagans, these days are the Sabbats, Esbats, and Astors. Sabbats are the days of the two solstices, the two equinoxes, and the four days that fall between these dates (the cross-quarter days). Esbats are the nights of the full moon, and Astors (my own name for these days) are the nights of the dark moon, when the stars can best be seen. The bulk of this book will focus on days that are special to Pagans because they are marked by the sacred cycles, but there are some days we all set aside as special because they are meant to celebrate something about our lives and culture. These are the days of celebration. These days can also be called holidays (or holy days) because of their significance. In this section, we will look at cultural and religious holidays and personal holidays, such as birthdays and anniversaries.

As Pagans have their holidays honoring sacred cycles, so do other religions recognize days that are special to their religion. Besides honoring our own holidays, you can also pay tribute to other religions by honoring their special days as well. Take some time to learn the stories and the reason for their particular celebrations. Understand each tradition from which it came. Each religious practice and its holidays teach us about different perspectives of ourselves and concepts of deity. There are also cultural or secular holidays celebrated by different countries and cultures. In the United States, some of these holidays include Mother's Day, or there are religious holidays that have taken on more of a secular celebration, such as St. Valentine's Day. Following are some of the major holidays of several world religions, as well as some American cultural holidays. Choose the ones that are significant to you or that you might want to incorporate into your list of special days.

Month	Date	Religion	Holiday	Significance
J **A** **N** **U** **A** **R** **Y**	1	cultural	New Year's Day	celebration of the new year
	6	Christian	Epiphany	appearance of Wise Men to Jesus
	3rd Monday	cultural	MLK Day	birth of Martin Luther King, Jr.
	varies	Islamic	Eid ul-Adha	feast of sacrifice and gifts to the hungry
F **E** **B** **R** **U** **A** **R** **Y**	varies on Tuesday	Cultural	Mardi Gras	secular revival of Shrove Tuesday
	1	Pagan	Imbolc	first signs of Spring
	2	cultural	Groundhog Day	the groundhog looks for signs of Spring
	varies	Chinese	New Year	celebration of the new year
	10	Islamic	Al-Hijra	celebration of the new year
	12	cultural	Lincoln's Day	birth of Abraham Lincoln
	14	cultural	Valentine's Day	celebration of love
	3rd Monday	cultural	Washington's birthday	birth of George Washington
M **A** **R** **C** **H**	varies	Jewish	Purim	celebration of victory over persecution
	17	cultural	St. Patrick's Day	honoring Irish customs
	21	Baha'i	Naw-Ruz	celebration of the new year
	21	Pagan	Ostara	Spring equinox

Month	Date	Religion	Holiday	Significance
A P R I L	varies	Jewish	Passover	celebration of escape from Egypt
	varies	Christian	Easter	Resurrection of Jesus
	1	cultural	April Fool's Day	honoring the trickster
	3	Jain	Mahavir	birthday of Lord Mahavira
	4	Buddhist	Buddha Day	birthday of Buddha
	4	Sikh	Baisakhi	founding of the Khalsa
	17	Hindu	Ugadi	the day Brahma created the universe
	18	Jewish	Yom HaSho'ah	rememberance of the Holocaust
M A Y	varies	Islamic	Mawlid an-Nabi	birth of Mohammed
	2nd Sunday	cultural	Mother's Day	honoring all mothers
	last Monday	cultural	Memorial Day	honoring the memory of war dead
	1	cultural	Worker's Day	honoring the workers of society
	1	Pagan	Beltane	cross-quarter day
	23	Baha'i	Declaration	Bab declares a new revelation
	varies	Christian	Pentecost	Holy Spirit descends on followers of Jesus

Month	Date	Religion	Holiday	Significance
JUNE	3rd Sunday	cultural	Father's Day	honoring all fathers
	14	cultural	Flag Day	
	16	Sikh		martyrdom of Guru Arjan Dev
	21	Pagan	Litha	Summer solstice
	30	Shinto	Oharaithe	great purification
	31	Buddhist	Dharma	Day of the first lecture by Buddha
JULY	4	cutural	Independence Day	America's independence from Britain
AUGUST	1	Pagan	Lammas	festival of harvest
	6	Hindu	Krishna Jayanti	birth of Lord Krishna
	15	Christian	Theotokos	death and resurrection of Mary
SEPTEMBER	varies	Jewish	Rosh Hashanah	Jewish New Year
	varies	Jewish	Yom Kippur	day of atonement
	varies	Jewish	Sukkot	season of rejoicing
	1st Monday	cultural	Labor Day	honoring all workers
	1	Sikh	First Parkash	installation of the Sikh Scriptures
	21	Pagan	Mabon	Fall equinox

MONTH	DATE	RELIGION	HOLIDAY	SIGNIFICANCE
O C T O B E R	14	Hindu	Durga Puja/ Navaratri	honoring the fertility goddess Durga
	20	Baha'i	Birth of the Bab	
	31	Pagan	Samhain	honoring the dead
	31	cultural	Halloween	secular celebration of All Hallow's Eve
N O V E M B E R	varies	Islamic	Ramadan	
	4th Thursday	cultural	Thanksgiving	
	12	Hindu	Diwali	New year and festival of lights
	12	Baha'i	Birth of Baha'u'llah	
D E C E M B E R	8	Buddhist	Bodhi Day	Buddha's realization of the 4 noble truths
	varies	Jewish	Hanukkah	Festival of Light
	22	Pagan	Yule	Winter solstice
	25	Christian	Christmas	birth of Jesus
	26	cultural	Kwanzaa	affirmation of African values

There are also days that are special only to you and your friends and family. These are birthdays and anniversaries. In the first 300 years of Christianity, birthdays were considered pagan (as in, non-Christian) and were, therefore, not celebrated. As people continued the celebration of the day of their birth against the Church's wishes, they eventually gave in and allowed the celebration. Birthdays are now days in the year when someone can receive gifts or special treatment. Some employers even allow people to take their birthdays as a day off from work. Birthdays are special days that are good for honoring yourself and to be with those who love you. They are also good times to look back over your life and assess where you have been and where you should go in the future. This is called a life assessment and is an excellent way to add even more meaning and purpose to your birthday. When doing such an assessment, be positive. Do not just look at the negative occurrences in your past. Take some time to really appreciate the wonderful things that have happened to you in your life and commit yourself to build your future upon those good experiences.

One practice that many Pagans have adopted on their birthday is to do a divinatory reading that helps to clarify the issues and opportunities that will come in the following year. Through tarot cards, runes, or other systems, you can seek cosmic wisdom to help you focus on your next year.

Anniversaries can also be special days. People celebrate the day on which they were married, bought a new house, or started a new company, for example. Each of these days can be days for fun. They can also be days of unique spiritual significance. Some Pagan anniversaries that you may want to celebrate include the day you dedicated yourself to a Pagan path, the day you helped form a Pagan meeting group, days that are significant to your particular deity, or any days on which you had a significant spiritual event occur.

Exercise 3: Days of Celebration

Consider your answers to the following questions. I've provided space for your answers, or you can write them in your journal or some other study guide.

1. What holidays are significant to you?

_____

_____

_____

_____

_____

2. What is the significance of your birthday?

_____

_____

_____

_____

3. What anniversaries are significant to you?

_____

_____

_____

_____

The Cycles of the Moon
Weeks

The changes in the appearance of the moon once held great significance to people all over the world. As we become a culture whose electric lights wash out the night sky, we pay less and less attention to the light of the moon. Though we may not notice it as much, the moon still holds an influence over us, as any gardener, emergency medical worker, or late-night police officer might tell you. As we have previously seen in the discussion of the quarters of the day, there are four phases of the moon: full, waning half, new, and waxing half. The moon completes its cycle of changing light about every 28 1/4 days. Those four phases are closely associated with the weeks so that, almost every seven days, the moon changes into the next quarter. Because our calendar is now solar, the days of the week do not always line up with the same moon phases, and our months are slightly longer than a lunar cycle, so that we can sometimes have a month with two full moons (the Blue Moon). Despite this, we can still observe the four weeks of every month as having the same cycle of four phases. The first week is the child of the month and is a good time for initiating new projects. The second week is the maiden/suitor and is a good time for making connections with others, especially in relation to your new projects. The third week is the mother/father phase. Here it is a good time to nurture any new projects and allow them to begin to grow and help others. The fourth week is the phase of the crone/sage. In this time you should begin to wrap up any projects and to observe and learn from their effects. The remainder of the month can be used as a time to take a break before the next cycle.

Exercise 4: Weeks

Consider your answers to the following questions. I've provided space for your answers, or you can write them in your journal or some other study guide.

1. What to you is the significance of each of the following weeks in a month?

First week.

_____

_____

_____

_____

Second week.

_____

_____

_____

_____

Third week.

_____

_____

_____

_____

Fourth week.

_____

_____

_____

_____

Days in the Week

Each day in the week also has its own significance. The division of the lunar month into four parts creates weeks comprising of seven days each. Seven has always been a very spiritual number, because it was once thought that the solar system had seven planets, each of which influenced our lives on Gaia in different ways. Originally, the seven days of the week were named after the seven planets. Thus, we can apply the significance of each planet to its corresponding day.

Sunday is the day of the sun. For this reason, it is considered a sacred day to many. For a long time, Sunday was significant to the ancient peoples who worshipped the sun. The sun represents the side of ourselves that we present to others and how we define ourselves. It is the part of us we call the ego. As the seventh day, it is the day of rest for Christians. For modern Pagans, it is significant that Sunday appears before Monday, the day of the moon. Sunday night becomes the union between the sun and moon. The moon represents the inner part of us. It relates to the inner emotions, our hopes and dreams, and how we care and nurture others. Monday, of course, is also the first day of the workweek and is often viewed with contempt for that reason. It is unfortunate that a day dedicated to the moon can be attributed such negative feelings, but our society often shuns the feminine aspect of life. Maybe if we looked at Monday as a day to begin again with our hopes and dreams, we could help improve our feelings toward this day.

Tuesday is the day of the planet Mars. Mars is the Roman god of war, but the Romans did, after all, enjoy expanding their empire. Hopefully, you will not need to look to the warlike aspect of Mars to find spiritual significance for the day. Instead, you can appreciate the great energy of this planet, as Tuesday is the day to apply that energy. Mars is also known as the god of fertility. You can use this energy when planting your garden. The energy of Mars can also be channeled into the areas of creativity and sexuality.

Wednesday is the day we honor the planet Mercury. Mercury is the god with small wings on his feet that he uses to fly as he deliveres messages to and from the gods. He is the god of travel and communication. He is also the god of boundaries and crossroads, and can be considered the trickster god as well. Use his energy to help you communicate to others, make important decisions, and find opportunities to laugh in the face of adversity.

Jupiter rules over Thursday. Jupiter is the Roman high god and represents a sense of personal and spiritual expansion. The energy of Jupiter can be used for enthusiasm, for being spontaneous, and for developing one's spirituality.

Friday is the day of Venus, the goddess of love. Venus and her attributes for love, relationships, and beauty are well known, thanks to her patronage through so many years of artistic renditions devoted to her. Creating and enjoying the arts is another attribute of Venus.

Saturday is the day attributed to the god Saturn. In Roman mythology, the god Saturn actually existed before the other gods. He was one of the giant Titans. Even though he was defeated, his influence remained in the minds of the Romans because he was such a fierce god. In Greece, he was called Chronos, which is where we get the term *chronology*. Chronos was the god of time. Time limits us and forces us to create restrictions and boundaries. Through time we recognize the cyclic nature of the universe. Saturn became the god of limitations and discipline. For Jews and some other religions, Saturday is a holy day—the day of the Sabbath that begins on the preceding evening when the sun goes down. For some, Saturday is the day to spend at home, catching up on housework or spending time with the family.

Exercise 5: Days in the Week

Consider your answers to the following questions. I've provided space here for your answers, or you can write them in your journal or some other study guide.

1. What to you is the significance of each of the days in a week?

_____

_____

_____

_____

_____

_____

_____

_____

_____

_____

Months

Each of the four weeks symbolically represents the four phases of the lunar month. It is only symbolic, because our solar calendar does not align with true lunar phases. You can still follow and honor the lunar cycles by observing the nightly changes of the moon's light. In general, the time between the full and the dark moon (the waning moon) is a time for clearing away negative influences in your life, and the waxing moon (when the light begins to return) is a time for bringing in positive influences. Pagans call the night of the full moon the Esbat. The word *Esbat* actually has the same meaning as the word *Sabbath*, from which we get our word for solar celebrations: *Sabbats.* We use the word *Esbat*, however, to differentiate between seasonal celebrations and lunar celebrations. During the Esbat, magick, divination, and ritual are often used to celebrate, honor, and receive inspiration from the moon. The dark moon is the best time to observe and honor the stars, so I call that time the *Astor*, which means "star." The stars represent the multitude of life and the wisdom of the universe.

In this chapter, we will examine additional significance that can be attributed to the full moons, keeping in mind that the other phases (the waxing half moon, the dark moon, and the waning half moon) will be used as times to mark the changes to the next full moon. You can use the time of the full moon to identify special days of significance for your Pagan practice. During these days or nights you can honor the cycles of the moon, the Goddess, or the feminine aspects of your practice. You can also add special activities to commemorate the full moon and its monthly appearance, attributing to it special meaning. During the dark moon you can meditate on what will be the special meaning and observance you will enact for the coming full moon. Each of the half moons can be used as a time to check in on the progress of your activity for that moon. There are many ways to connect deeper meanings to each of the full moons. The methods we will examine are agricultural, celebratory, astrological, and chance.

People, once in tune with the phases of the moon and the seasons, named the full moons according to events that were common during that time of the year. Their significance, then, was closely associated with these natural changes. Nowadays, we can associate at least one full moon per calendar month (because there are 13 full moons in a year, though, some months are going to have two full moons). The second of these two full moons is called the Blue Moon, which has its own special significance.

There is no definitive version of what each of the new moons may have been called in the past, because each area would have named the different moons according to events related to that area. For example, when I lived in Vermont, we used to call the March moon the Sugar Moon, because that was the month when the maple syrup ran. It would not make sense to call the March moon the Sugar Moon in Florida, though. Though the moons are related to seasonal events, each can be given significance related to correlations between Gaia changes and changes in the human condition. Here are some ways in which each of the moons can be given spiritual significance based on common names. You, of course, can change the names of each of the moons to suit your own seasonal and spiritual needs.

• • • • • • •

Month: January
Name: Cold Moon
Seasonal Significance: Time to ration food and energy to
                                survive the Winter
Spiritual Significance: Time to rest and reserve energy

• • • • • • •

Month: February
Name: Quickening Moon
Seasonal Significance: First birth of some animals
Spiritual Significance: Time to plan for new projects

• • • • • • •

Month: March
Name: Storm Moon
Seasonal Significance: First plantings; great weather
                                changes
Spiritual Significance: Time to sow seeds and foster
                                growth

• • • • • • •

Month: April
Name: Wind Moon
Seasonal Significance: First growth
Spiritual Significance: Time to nurture projects and
                                others

• • • • • • •

Month: May
Name: Flower Moon
Seasonal Significance: First blooms
Spiritual Significance: Time to enjoy and share beauty

• • • • • • •

Month: June
Name: Long Days Moon
Seasonal Significance: Beginning of the long, hot days of
                    Summer
Spiritual Significance: Time to enjoy the days

• • • • • • •

Month: July
Name: Honey Moon
Seasonal Significance: Time to collect honey
Spiritual Significance: Time for spiritual unions

• • • • • • •

Month: August
Name: Corn Moon
Seasonal Significance: First harvest
Spiritual Significance: Time to finish projects

• • • • • • •

Month: September
Name: Harvest Moon
Seasonal Significance: Second harvest
Spiritual Significance: Time to collect what you need and
                    distribute extras

• • • • • • •

Month: October

Name: Blood Moon

Seasonal Significance: Slaughter of animals for Winter
                                food

Spiritual Significance: Time to remember and honor the
                                dead

• • • • • • •

Month: November

Name: Remembrance Moon

Seasonal Significance: Last chance to feast on Summer
                                harvests

Spiritual Significance: Time to honor your gifts and
                                blessings

• • • • • • •

Month: December

Name: Long Nights Moon

Seasonal Significance: Beginning of the cold days of
                                Winter

Spiritual Significance: Time for rest and storing up
                                personal energy

• • • • • • •

Month: One with a second full moon

Name: Blue Moon

Seasonal Significance: Varies

Spiritual Significance: Time for divination and magick

• • • • • • •

Month	Holidays of Inspiration	Moon
January	New Year's Day	Hibernation
February	Valentine's Day	Love
March	St. Patrick's Day, Mardi Gras, Purim	Tolerance, Purification
April	Easter, April Fool's Day, Buddha Day	Honesty
May	Worker's Day, Mother's Day, Memorial Day	Mother or Goddess
June	Father's Day, Dharma Day	Father or God
July	Independence Day	Liberty
August	Birth of Krishna	Wisdom
September	Rosh Hoshanah, Labor Day, First Parkash	Forgiveness
October	Halloween	Ancestor
November	Thanksgiving	Gratitude
December	Christmas	Family

Another way to apply significance to the full moons is by relating them to other festivals or celebrations of the same month. For example, January is a month of few holidays, and for good reason. The number of holidays during the month of December would seem to indicate that the Winter solstice was an important and busy time of the year for many different religious traditions. It makes sense, then, that the cold period following the solstice would be a time of less activity. It is important to conserve energy in the Winter. The moon in January could be called the Hibernation Moon. February is the month in which the secular holiday of Valentine's Day appears. This holiday has become a time to express your love and dedication to a special someone. Despite its origins as a way to sell more greeting cards, it is a worthy thing to honor and celebrate your love to others. The full moon in February could be related to Valentine's Day and be labeled the Love Moon. The previous page is a chart of full moons and possible relationships to holidays during the same month, not including Pagan Sabbats.

If a month contains two full moons, the second is called a Blue Moon and is considered a good moon for working magick or other spiritual workings.

Once again, you can see how each moon can represent a variety of things. The important thing is to find holidays that have special significance to you and then use them as inspiration for what the moon of that month should represent.

Another interesting way of attributing significance to the moons is through an astrological system. This method takes into account that each full moon appears within one of the 12 Zodiac signs every month. Each sign of the Zodiac has the qualities of one of the four elements and one of

the three virtues (called cardinal, fixed, and mutable). These three virtues are attributes of how energy is applied to any activity. When energy
is first applied, it is called *cardinal* (meaning first). As the energy enters
into the event and stabilizes itself, it is called *fixed*. When the event is
drawing to a close, the energy is withdrawn, leaving open the possibility
for future change. This stage is called *mutable*. You can also envision this
energy in terms of the forces we discussed in Chapter 2. Cardinal energy
is the same as Expressive energy—that is, the force of individuation or
moving away from the source. Fixed energy is the force of Balance between Expression and Envelopment. Mutable energy is the force of Envelopment that calls one back to the source of all: Spirit. The Zodiac
signs also have qualities of their own, and most people know these through
their sun signs. You can attach meaning to the full moons using which-
ever of these methods you wish. I am going to focus upon using the elements and the virtues. Refer to the chart on page 135 for the Zodiac signs
with their qualities.

Yet another method for attributing significance to the full moons is
through the process of chance possible through divination. With this system, you would use a selected divination tool, such as the runes or tarot
cards. You would need to determine significance for each card or item in
your divination system. Then, with each full moon, you would pull a card,
rune stone, or other item and determine how it would relate to that particular moon. As an example, I will use the tarot cards. In this system,
there are cards with numbers and four suits (Disks, Swords, Wands, and
Cups). These cards are the Minor Arcana. There is a set of cards that
also uses the four suits but has royal figures on them. These are called the
Court Cards. There is another group of cards called the Major Arcana
that contain roman numerals and words. You can relate the four suits of

Sign	Element	Virtue	Significance
Aries	Fire	Cardinal	Expressive energy for the heart
Taurus	Earth	Fixed	Balanced energy for the body
Gemini	Air	Mutable	Enfolding energy for the mind
Cancer	Water	Cardinal	Expressive energy for the soul
Leo	Fire	Fixed	Balanced energy for the heart
Virgo	Earth	Mutable	Enfolding energy for the body
Libra	Air	Cardinal	Expressive energy for the mind
Scorpio	Water	Fixed	Balanced energy for the soul
Sagittarius	Fire	Mutable	Enfolding energy for the heart
Capricorn	Earth	Cardinal	Expressive energy for the body
Aquarius	Air	Fixed	Balanced energy for the mind
Pisces	Water	Mutable	Enfolding energy for the soul

the minor arcana to the four elements (Disks = Earth, Swords = Air, Wands = Fire, Cups = Water), the numbers to the 10 planets, and the Court Cards to people. The Major cards are related to Spirit. For a listing of possible attributes, I will use the Waite-Smith Tarot Deck. (Though it is usually called the Rider-Waite deck, I prefer to call it the Waite-Smith to honor the woman who designed the artwork for the cards.)

	Major Arcana Cards (Waite-Smith Deck)	
Number	**Card**	**Significance**
0	The Fool	Beginning or exploring a new spiritual journey
I	The Magician	Seeking the God
II	The High Priestess	Seeking the Goddess
III	The Empress	Honoring mother or mother figure
IV	The Emperor	Honoring father or father figure
V	The Heirophant	Teaching or helping one to change
VI	The Lovers	Expressing and experiencing love
VII	The Chariot	Finding a direction or taking control
VIII	Strength	Breaking through interference
IX	The Hermit	Seeking introspection and silence
X	Wheel of Fortune	Seeking flexibility or a needed change
XI	Justice	Seeking fairness and understanding
XII	The Hanged Man	Offering sacrifice or taking a different view
XIII	Death	Ending something
XIV	Temperance	Seeking a balance between forces
XV	The Devil	Seeking humor or pleasure
XVI	The Tower	Changing an old habit
XVII	The Star	Seeking wisdom and learning
XVIII	The Moon	Pursuing a dream
XIX	The Sun	Seeking growth or Expression
XX	Judgment	Making a firm decision
XXI	The World	Finding a way to gain wholeness and unity

\multicolumn{4}{c}{Minor Arcana Cards}			
NUMBER	**PLANET**	**KEYWORDS**	**SIGNIFICANCE** (RELATED TO SUIT)
Ace	Sun	Strength, self	Strength to body, mind, heart, or soul
2	Moon	Change, dreams	Change to body, mind, heart, or soul
3	Mercury	Creation, Expression	Expression for body, mind, heart, or soul
4	Saturn	Home, limitations	Rest for body, mind, heart, or soul
5	Mars	Energy, dominance	Energy to body, mind, heart, or soul
6	Venus	Relationships, love	Connection through body, mind, heart, or soul
7	Jupiter	Expansion, spirituality	Expansion of body, mind, heart, or soul
8	Pluto	Rebirth, renewal, endings	Renewal of body, mind, heart, or soul
9	Neptune	Intuition, completion	Inspiration for body, mind, heart, or soul
10	Uranus	New direction, independence	New direction for body, mind, heart, or soul
Page		Young female	Influence of young female with Earth, Air, Fire, or Water characteristics
Knight		Young male	Influence of young male with Earth, Air, Fire, or Water characteristics
Queen		Older female	Influence of older female with Earth, Air, Fire, or Water characteristics
King		Older male	Influence of older male with Earth, Air, Fire, or Water characteristics

137

Exercise 6: Months

Consider your answers to the following questions. I've provided space here for your answers, or you can write them in your journal or some other study guide.

1. What to you is the significance of each of the full moons of the 12 months?

    _____

    _____

    _____

    _____

    _____

    _____

    _____

    _____

    _____

    _____

2. What to you is the significance of the Blue Moon?

    _____

    _____

    _____

The Cycles of the Sun

The Sabbats

Similar to the moon, the sun also appears to go through several phases. Because of the rotation of Gaia, we experience the cycle of the day with its motion from light to dark. As Gaia also travels around the sun, we experience greater or lesser degrees of light during the day, depending on the season and what part of the globe we live on. Because our world is tilted on its axis, we encounter varying degrees of light and heat, creating two phases to the year. From the Winter solstice to the Summer solstice, the sun's light appears to be waxing. After the Summer solstice, the light of the sun appears to be waning. Thus, as with the moon, we undergo the phases of the waning and waxing sun marked by the solstices. The word *solstice* means a time when the sun stands still. Each day on the horizon, the sun appears to set at a slightly different location until it reaches the solstice point, where it appears not to move for three days. After the solstice, the sun appears again to move in the opposite direction across the horizon. People began to figure out that the point midway between the waxing sun was a good time to sow seeds, and that the midpoint of the waning sun was a good time to harvest the plants. For modern Pagans, the waxing sun is a good time for planting seeds, beginning projects, or offering our energy to good works, and the waning sun is a good time for gathering together the result of our work, seeking rest and introspection, or collecting things for those in need. The seasons, then, became a way to mark the changes in the cycle of a single year.

Because we tend to live for many years, we can also recognize multiple year cycles. We celebrate decades and centuries. Birthdays and years that are multiples of 10 have more significance than others. The recent fear that we all experienced when the new century was upon us stands as a good example.

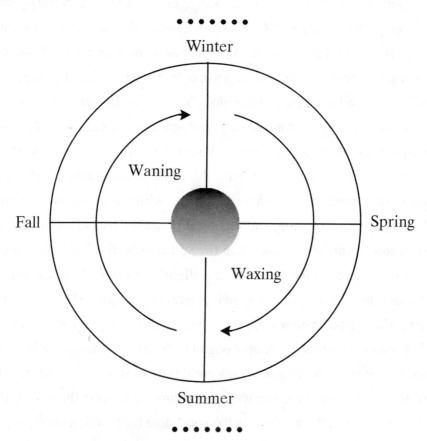

The midpoint day between the solstices became known as the equinox, which means equal time. On these days, the amount of daylight is balanced between the amount of darkness and light (depending on where you live, of course). With the two solstices and the two equinoxes, we get the four seasons: Winter, Spring, Fall, and Summer. Because the light of the sun actually reaches us more quickly than the heat of the sun, each of the four days marks the beginning of a season rather than the middle.

Because these days had such an impact on the lives of people, it was only natural that they become spiritual holy days. At some point, people started also celebrating the points between these days and marked them as the height of each season. Pagans now reclaim all these days as sacred and call them the days of the Wheel of the Year. The specific days are now called Sabbats. The eight Sabbats help us celebrate the cyclic nature of Gaia and Her travels around the sun. Through them we come to understand the circle of life and rebirth. Many myths developed around the pattern of the seasons and the year. One such story is the myth of the dying and reborn god, which is the representation of the sun. In this myth, the god is born after the Winter solstice, grows up and joins with the Goddess Gaia to awaken life at the Spring equinox, then grows to full strength at the Summer solstice. After the Summer solstice, the god then begins to decline until after the Fall equinox, when he dies. The Goddess is saddened and mourns his death until the Winter solstice, when he is again reborn and the cycle continues anew.

Because the circle of the seasons bears resemblance to the ritual circle, Pagans relate the two by assigning a correspondence of the seasons to the four elements. Spring is related to Air because of the airiness and lightness of the season. Summer is related to Fire because of the heat of the sun. Fall is related to Water because of the great rains and the upcoming snow. Earth is related to Winter because of the barren earth that is exposed during this season. I have also added elemental relationships to the cross-quarter days in order to balance waxing Sabbats with waning Sabbats. For example, the two waxing seasons are Winter and Spring, which relate to Earth and Air, respectively. In order to allow Earth and Air to appear on the waning side of the Wheel of the Year, I have attributed them to the two cross-quarter days on that side of the circle. The following puts all these attributes of the cycle of the sun together for the eight Sabbats. (Dates are approximate.)

• • • • • • •

Sabbat:	Yule
Date:	December 21
Sun Phase:	Waxing
Element:	Earth
Season:	Beginning of Winter
Agricultural Event:	Rationing food and fuel for the Winter
Significance:	The sowing of the body

• • • • • • •

Sabbat:	Imbolc
Date:	February 1
Sun Phase:	Waxing
Element:	Fire
Season:	Height of Winter
Agricultural Event:	Some animals begin to produce milk
Significance:	The sowing of the heart

• • • • • • •

Sabbat: Ostara

Date: March 21

Sun Phase: Waxing

Element: Air

Season: Beginning of Spring

Agricultural Event: Life is renewed; planting begins

Significance: The sowing of the mind

• • • • • • •

Sabbat: Beltane

Date: May 1

Sun Phase: Waxing

Element: Water

Season: Height of Spring

Agricultural Event: Second planting begins

Significance: The sowing of the soul

• • • • • • •

Sabbat: Litha

Date: June 21

Sun Phase: Waning

Element: Fire

Season: The beginning of Summer

Agricultural Event: Plants grow; fruits are collected

Significance: The harvest of the heart

• • • • • • •

Sabbat: Lammas

Date: August 1

Sun Phase: Waning

Element: Earth

Season: Height of Summer

Agricultural Event: The first harvest of crops

Significance: The harvest of the body

• • • • • • •

Sabbat: Mabon

Date: September 21

Sun Phase: Waning

Element: Water

Season: Fall

Agricultural Event: The second harvest of crops

Significance: The harvest of the soul

• • • • • • •

Sabbat: Samhain

Date: October 31

Sun Phase: Waning

Element: Air

Season: Height of Fall

Agricultural Event: The final harvest

Significance: The harvest of the mind

• • • • • • •

Exercise 7: The Sabbats

Consider your answers to the following questions. I've provided space here for your answers, or you can write them in your journal or some other study guide.

1. What to you is the significance of each of the eight Sabbats?

_____

_____

_____

_____

_____

_____

_____

The Septenary

We have observed a single year cycle of the Gaia's revolution around the sun. There are also longer cycles that affect our lives. One of these cycles is the pattern of seven years—the septenary. We have already discussed the significance of the 28 days in the lunar cycle and how this was divided into four segments of seven to create the week. Every seven days, the moon changes from one phase to the next, and it takes 14 days for the moon to change from full to its exact opposite (the dark moon). The same number is also significant in terms of human years. Every 14 years we go through a significant life change. Every seven years, then, is half of that cycle.

For many religious traditions, the number seven has always held special significance. Pythagoreans called seven the union of the square (the mundane) and the triangle (the spiritual). Many religious pantheons list seven main deities. In the tradition of the Abrahamic religions, the world was created in six days and an additional day (the seventh) was used for rest. *Sabbath* is a word that means "seventh," and is a name used to designate that special day of rest. Today, Pagans use a derivation of that word to name our significant days, the *Sabbats*, which come about every six to seven weeks in the year. In the Christian tradition, there are seven sacraments that are important in life. The symbol of the cross is an intersection of four units with three units. The African-American tradition of Kwanzaa holds dear seven principles. In Hindu philosophy, there are seven main energy centers in the body called *chakras*. These are but just a few of the examples of the recurrence of the sacred number seven. Then, of course, there are the seven planets.

People once believed that when a child is born its soul comes from the realm of the stars and travels through the spheres of the seven planets before it enters its new body. This is how the planets are believed to affect our lives at birth. The second part of the theory holds that our purpose in life is to symbolically work our way back through the influence of the planets and return to the realm of the stars. A seven-year cycle of spiritual work, called a *septenary*, is one way to enact this process. If you assign to each year the influence of one of the seven planets and then use that year to work through spiritual challenges based on the influence of that planet, you can begin a seven-year cycle of spiritual development that is a profound, deep, and meaningful way to commit your life to Pagan practice. For those interested in this work, I have created a chart (see page 147) of the seven planets, their keywords, and their

YEAR	PLANET	KEYWORD	THE BODY: Parts of the Body	THE MIND: Areas of Study	THE HEART: Relationships	THE SOUL: Virtues
1	Sun	Strength, self	Head	Natural sciences	Self	Fortitude/ courage
2	Moon	Change, dreams	Back	Fine arts	Lovers	Hope
3	Mercury	Creation, Expression	Stomach	Communication	Children	Justice
4	Venus	Relationships, love	Chest	Social sciences	Female relatives	Love, charity
5	Mars	Energy, resolution	Sexual region	Performing arts	Male relatives	Practicality
6	Jupiter	Expansion, spirituality	Hands/ arms	Meta-physics	Friends	Faith
7	Saturn	Home, limitations	Legs/feet	Math	Enemies	Moderation

relationships to the four elements and parts of the self. The addition of the relationship to the elements is to help facilitate connection to other cycles throughout the year. This allows you to define a general theme for the year and then refine that theme through other cycles, such as monthly and daily cycles. For the element of Earth (the body), I have listed seven parts of the body. For the element of Air (the mind), I have included seven areas of study. The element of Fire (the heart) is related to seven relationships, and the element of Water (the soul) is related to seven virtues or ways of seeking Spirit.

Exercise 8: The Septenary

Consider your answers to the following questions. I've provided space here for your answers, or you can write them in your journal or some other study guide.

1. What to you is the significance of each of the following years of the seven-year cycle?

First year.

_____

_____

_____

_____

_____

_____

_____

Second year.

_____

_____

_____

_____

_____

_____

Third year.

_____

_____

_____

_____

_____

_____

Fourth year.

_____

_____

_____

_____

_____

Fifth year.

_____

_____

_____

_____

_____

Sixth year.

_____

_____

_____

_____

_____

Seventh year.

_____

_____

_____

_____

_____

The Cycles of Life

The seventh year is also significant in longer cycles that affect our lives. These are the cycles of life: changes that all people go through in their journey from birth to death. Ancient wisdom proclaimed that there were seven periods that marked the major changes in our lives, each of which is derived from multiples of seven. After birth, the first period is marked at seven months, when the baby begins teething. After 14 months, the baby sits up straight, marking the second period. The third period occurs at 21 months, when the baby begins to walk. At 28 months, the baby learns to speak, and the baby ceases sucking after 35 months. The sixth stage happens at 14 years, when the child enters adulthood, and the seventh stage takes place at the age of 21, when growing ceases. Though this particular view of the importance of the number seven in life ended at this final stage, significant changes continue to happen in our lives afterwards. These stages are part of the Wheel of Life.

As does the Wheel of the Year, the Wheel of Life recognizes that all life is cyclic. In youth, our bodies grow in strength and energy, and then we begin to lose that youthful energy as we age. We come from the mystery of Spirit, we grow through and with its energy, and then we release that energy to, once again, return to the mystery of Spirit. Through that journey, we encounter specific changes in our lives that cause us to reexamine our relationship with ourselves, with others, and with the universe. I believe that every seven years we go through important changes in our lives, and that each of these stages has a major life event associated with these changes that can be celebrated.

We have observed the four faces of the Goddess and Her relationship to the moon, sun, and Gaia cycles. These same faces can be seen in the life cycle as well. The first 14 years of life is the stage of the child, when we learn about the world. The next 14 years of life is the stage of the maiden or suitor, when we come to define our relationship with others and search for a mate. The next cycle, that of the father or mother, is longer and lasts 28 years. At this time in our lives, we take on the responsibilities of work and caring for others. Whether or not we actually have our own children does not matter. We all come to take on a part of the shared work of being a cooperative society, helping all our children to learn and grow. The stage of the crone or sage is the final stage of life. During this time we share our great wisdom and experience with others, and are released from our responsibilities to society so that we can use our last years to explore and expand our spiritual relationship. Each of these four phases contains within it seven-year sub-stages. Each sub-stage contains a type of celebration that can be celebrated during that stage. The chart on page 153 lists all of these stages.

The Child Phase

In the first seven years of life, the baby is wholly dependent upon its caregivers for life and protection. In some religious communities, this is also the time when the parents commit to raising their child within their specific tradition. Pagans believe strongly that each individual has the right to choose his or her own spiritual practice. Though we may not feel it is right to commit the child to one particular religion, we can make a commitment to raise him or her within our own spiritual path, if only to offer the child a base from which to be supported as he or she grows. The child will be free to choose any religious path when he or she is ready, but, until then, you can have a spiritual framework within which you can support him or her.

STAGE	SUB-STAGE	AGE	SIGNIFICANCE
Child	Baby	1–6	A new dependent being is created
	Young child	7–13	The child becomes independent
Maiden/Suitor	Teen	14–20	The child seeks a mate
	Young adult	21–27	The adult flees the nest
Mother/Father	Adult	28–34	The person develops full strength
	Mid-life	35–41	The person hears life's calling
	Menopause	42–48	The person takes account of her life
	The jubilee	49–55	Preparation for final stage is made
Crone/Sage	Senior	56–62	Time for life's fulfillment
	Retirement	63–69	One is released from work
	The return	70–	One prepares for death
	Death		

At age 7, the baby becomes a young child and is able to slowly begin to define himself or herself and become somewhat self-sufficient. This age is marked by the loss of the baby teeth. This event can become a significant factor in the growth of a child who seeks to be recognized as more than a baby. Our culture has a tradition of putting a tooth under the child's pillow and then exchanging it for money before the next morning. We use the story of the tooth fairy to add a bit of magick to the event. The origin of this tradition comes from the idea that a part of a person's body (such as the hair or teeth) can be used by someone else to control them. So, it was important to protect these things and keep them away from others. By putting a tooth under a pillow, you protect it from being stolen at night. A benevolent fairy takes away the tooth, making it impossible for someone else to use it.

Exercise 9: The Child Phase

Consider your answers to the following questions. I've provided space here for your answers, or you can write them in your journal or some other study guide.

1. What to you is the significance of the baby stage?

_____

_____

_____

_____

_____

_____

2. What to you is the significance of the young child stage?

_____

_____

_____

_____

_____

_____

The Maiden/Suitor Phase

Almost all religions recognize the importance of the age of 14 (or thereabouts) as the time when children are no longer children. Girls begin the menses cycle, and both boys and girls begin to grow new hair. Whether you call them adolescents, teens, or something else, you recognize that they are experiencing the world in a different way. This is the time when young people begin defining their own selves and their world through other groups and people. At this stage, many people also begin looking for the special relationship of a mate.

At 21, the person truly becomes a young adult. This is the time when the young person often leaves home to begin study or a life of his or her own. Usually the need to find a mate becomes more serious, and this can be the time for making a commitment to another person and to a new life.

Exercise 10: The Maiden/Suitor Phase

Consider your answers to the following questions. I've provided space for your answers, or you can write them in your journal or some other study guide.

1. What to you is the significance of the teen stage?

    _____

    _____

    _____

    _____

    _____

2. What to you is the significance of the young adult stage?

    _____

    _____

    _____

    _____

    _____

The Mother/Father Phase

The stage of mother/father is longer than the previous two stages. Growth takes place less rapidly. Changes become more about relationships with each other than about the physical body. Around the age of 28, the young adult becomes a full-fledged adult, as his or her body develops into full strength. At this point in life, the adult learns to become responsible for the care and love of others—especially children. Though it used to be at a younger age, many people now wait until this stage of life to make a lifelong commitment to someone through marriage. This can also be the time when the couple decides to have or become guardians for children, offering the chance to perform birthing and naming ceremonies. Approaching the age of 35 is often called the time of mid-life, and it is here that some experience the infamous mid-life crisis. This particular challenge in life calls us to take a look at our past and the influence we may have had upon the world. This is also the time for many when they hear the calling to a stronger spiritual understanding of the universe. Many people try to ignore this spiritual crisis, but I believe we should honor and use this opportunity to help us come to terms with this time of reckoning and spiritual calling.

For women, the next stage, starting around the age of 42, is marked by a physical change called menopause. Men's bodies also change, but not to the same extent as women. At this stage, the body is no longer able to produce children and hormonal changes take place within the body. At age 49, a person has reached the seventh of the seven-year cycles, and this is, indeed, an auspicious event. There is an interesting Hebrew custom of old called the Jubilee. The year after seven cycles of seven years (50 years) is proclaimed as the year of the Jubilee. In this year, all debts, sins, and feuds are forgiven. It is a time of great celebration and a chance to start over again; spiritual vows and commitments are renewed.

Exercise 11: The Mother/Father Phase

Consider your answers to the following questions. I've provided space here for your answers, or you can write them in your journal or some other study guide.

1. What to you is the significance of the adult stage?

_____

_____

_____

2. What to you is the significance of the mid-life stage?

_____

_____

_____

_____

_____

3. What to you is the significance of the menopause stage?

_____

_____

_____

_____

_____

4. What to you is the significance of the Jubilee stage?

_____

_____

_____

_____

_____

The Crone/Sage Phase

At the age of 56, we enter the stage of senior citizen and are recognized as such by the number of stores that give discounts. Though everyone likes to save money, few in our society experience the distinction of senior citizen with honor. That is because our society values youth and newness rather than experience and wisdom. Many earlier societies honored their elders and looked to them to help the community learn and grow. The younger members of the society especially valued the spiritual teachings of those who had walked the path before them. Despite the pressures of our culture, I hope you will come to value your later years in life and take the time to share your wisdom with others as a great crone or sage. Unfortunately, many young people look on the elderly as weak and senile. In a way, this attitude creates a self-fulfilling prophecy. Because older people are not honored, they begin to feel useless and lifeless. Without this sense of value and worth, they become depressed and illness is allowed to settle in. Of course, an aging body will begin to display weaknesses, but we know that the mind and its attitudes are an important part of good health. We create circles of influence through our attitudes. If we value our seniors, they will feel valued and will, then, become of value.

At 63, it is time to make preparations for retirement and the event that marks this stage of life: the retirement party. This should be a joyous celebration that honors the time when work responsibilities are ending and a chance for free exploration can begin. At 70, it is time to consider one's end of life, or the return. The final stage of life is, of course, death itself.

Exercise 12: The Crone/Sage Phase

Consider your answers to the following questions. I've provided space for your answers, or you can write them in your journal or some other study guide.

1. What to you is the significance of the senior stage?

   _____

   _____

   _____

   _____

2. What to you is the significance of the retirement stage?

   _____

   _____

   _____

   _____

3. What to you is the significance of the return stage?

   _____

   _____

   _____

   _____

   _____

4. What to you is the significance of the death stage?

   _____

   _____

   _____

   _____

   _____

A Summary of Cycles

Now that that you have examined all the many sacred cycles in detail and have been given several methods to honor these cycles, it is time to determine which cycles are important to you and what the significance of each should be. Create a list of the cycles you wish to incorporate into your practice. As before, it is not necessary that you practice with all of the cycles all at once. Create a long-term goal for yourself to help you create a way of living your Pagan values through these sacred cycles.

4

Merging Goals and Cycles

Introduction

Up to this point we have observed four categories of spiritual goals: developing the self, helping others, honoring Gaia and Spirit, and honoring yourself and others; and four categories of natural cycles: Gaia cycles, such as the days; moon cycles, such as the weeks and months; sun cycles, such as Sabbats and other special days of the year; and multiple year cycles called *septenaries* and *life cycles*. Now we will learn how to combine those spiritual goals that you have identified as important to you from Chapter 2 with the cycles of the universe and of life you have chosen to honor from Chapter 3. Each of the four categories can be joined together to make a complete practice. Observe the chart on page 164.

Cycle	Goal
Gaia	Honoring Gaia and Spirit, and other daily practices
Moon	Developing the self
Sun	Helping others
Life	Honoring yourself and others

The first two categories are personal; the second two are more group-oriented. Through Gaia and Moon cycles, you engage in personal practices of gratitude and growth as well as those practices you have determined in earlier chapters that need to be done on a daily basis. Even though these practices include your interactions with others, they are primarily personal in their intent. The sun and life cycles are better celebrated within a spiritual community, such as a coven, Pagan learning circle, or other regular meeting group. These are cycles that support and honor others. They may include times to honor yourself, but are done in mutually expressive ways. In the same way that you need growth, development, and support found in the first two types of cycles, you can offer these same things to others through the second two types of cycles. As you celebrate life changes and seek to fulfill needs, you learn to do the same for others.

To combine goals with cycles, you need to decide which cycles relate to which goals. In Pagan traditions, Esbats are shared among small groups of people, such as in a coven. In my own practice, the Astor is a more personal ritual. Sabbats, on the other hand, are large group ceremonies. In our daily cycles, we are provided with ample opportunities to offer and accept blessings for all the little gifts of life we receive from Gaia and Spirit. Throughout our lives, we are also given opportunities to celebrate the many changes in life we experience and that we can share with others. You can use the daily cycles of Gaia to honor the blessings given to you by both Gaia and Spirit. The Moon cycles can be used to help you make improvements in your life and to yourself through the four elements. Sun cycles are a great time to come together with your spiritual community to celebrate Sabbats and other special days, and to use these days to join together to help others, whereas life cycles offer you, your friends, and spiritual companions a chance to jointly celebrate the life changes in each other.

To put it all together, you would need to do the following: Devise a daily plan, create and use a special calendar, and establish meanings and practices for regular and special days. The daily plan will include the regular events of the four parts of the day and the ways in which you can honor Gaia and Spirit. You will also need to consider special events or days that come up through the observance of other cycles. These could include special days of the week or month, Esbats, Astors, Sabbats, birthdays, anniversaries, holidays, and other special days. Birthdays will need to be given special consideration, depending on which stage of life will be celebrated, so the specific type of birthday should be noted as well. If you are following the septenary plan, you will also need to identify the themes for the particular year. Finally, for each of your spiritual activities during the day and for each special or religious day, you will need to decide exactly how you will honor and worship the significance of that day. In this chapter we will take a look at some ways in which goals and cycles can be combined. I will offer you only one of a multitude of ways of how these things can be put together, and it is my hope that you will find the method that works best for you.

Gaia Cycles and Honoring Gaia and Spirit

With every day of your life, you can come to honor Gaia and Spirit in simple yet meaningful ways. You can also use each day as an opportunity to put more magick and meaning into your life. Each day you are given a chance to start over again, and it is up to you how you will determine who you will be for that day. In this section, we will examine each part of the day and see how specific spiritual practices can be added to the Pagan life.

The Dawn

From midnight to 6 a.m. is the time when many of us are sleeping. It would seem that there would not be much else to do during this time, but there are a couple of things we can consider about our sleep time. One important thing that can often be overlooked is the importance of getting a good night's sleep. Sleeping well is an important part of good health and well-being. If you spend the day being tired, it will be that much more difficult to find the energy to do your work and enjoy your life. I believe that we sleep because it is a necessary way for us to remain connected to Gaia and Spirit. After all, we are usually lying down and, in effect, hugging Gaia. Make your time of sleep a sacred time, and the place where you sleep equally sacred. Prepare for bed in a way that honors the gifts of rest and sleep.

We can also use the nightly gift of dreaming as a spiritual act. Dreaming is a great way to listen to your inner self and to the wisdom of Spirit.

Encourage yourself to listen to your dreams and to write them down when you first awake. Don't be too anxious to interpret the dreams at first. Simply write them down for at least a month. Then consult dream dictionaries or, better yet, let the symbols in the dreams speak directly to you. Look for repeated images and recurring patterns. Let your sleeping mind be open to seeing the symbols and hearing messages.

Exercise 1: The Dawn

Consider your answers to the following questions. I've provided space here for your answers, or you can write them in your journal or some other study guide.

1. Which of your spiritual goals can best be done in the dawn of each day?

_____

_____

_____

_____

_____

2. How will you practice these goals?

_____

_____

_____

_____

_____

The Morning

EVENT	GOAL	PRACTICE
Wake	Honoring yourself	Positive visualization for the day
Wake	Soulful Enveloping	Meditation
Breakfast	Honoring Gaia	Blessing the meal
After breakfast	Honoring Gaia/ Physical Expression	Taking a walk
Going to work (or gathering)	Honoring Gaia	Observing beauty
Beginning work	Honoring Spirit	Positive energy for work
At work (or gathering)	Honoring Spirit	Practicing honest communication
At work (or gathering)	Honoring Spirit	Offering praise and thanks
At work (or gathering)	Honoring Spirit	Practicing ethics
At work (or gathering)	Honoring Spirit	Practicing empathy and compassion

From when you first wake to noon can be a very busy time—especially during the weekdays when work, school, and family all need your attention. Once again, though, you can allow different parts of your busy day to provide chances to practice your spirituality. The first important time comes when you first awaken. Often, the attitudes and feelings you develop at this important time can affect the rest of your day. Take note of how you approach each day. As the fog of sleep begins to clear (and after you have written down your dreams), your mind begins to focus on the coming day. There is an opportunity to take this time to frame a positive and magickal viewpoint for your whole day. Seize that chance and consider the special gift of being given another day of life and another chance to do right and live well. If you don't even consider that possibility, you will be eliminating your chances to discover it.

The morning is also a good time to practice some form of active or passive meditation—even if it's only for a short time. Through meditation you can encourage relaxation and an open mind, and be aware of your body for the day. Meditation also allows you another chance to listen to your inner self or to the wisdom of Spirit. Through relaxing your body, slowing your breath, and focusing on thoughts of peace and compassion, you can make it possible to carry these things through your day. The morning is also the time for the first meal. Eating is yet another way in which you remain connected to Gaia and Spirit. As you eat, you consume gifts from Gaia and from the work of others. You can be thankful for these things by offering a small prayer or blessing to these sources of your nourishment. Eating is also a time to enjoy the sensual pleasures of food. Instead of stuffing your breakfast down your throat as fast as possible, take a few short moments to enjoy the taste and smell of your food. If possible, you could use the morning time to take a healthy walk in nature for exercise and for the chance to get your body moving through exercise.

The morning is also the time when most of us leave home and take part in some form of social interaction. During the weekdays, the form of social interaction for many people is work. Even for those who may work at home, there is almost always some form of interaction with other people involved. On the weekends or during off times, social interaction may take different forms. People may be involved in amateur sports or entertainment activities, or a variety of other things that involve getting together with family and friends. For many, some form of regular social interaction is a large part of their life, and it only stands to reason that finding a way to live spiritually must include these activities as well. For now, I will talk about what can be done at work, but many of my suggestions could apply to other forms of interaction as well.

Beginning the workday often involves taking some form of transportation from home to the place of work. This trip can be viewed as either a necessary inconvenience or as yet another opportunity to connect to Spirit. The drive or ride to work is a unique opportunity for quieting the mind and preparing for the coming activities. Instead of doing something to occupy your mind, try sitting quietly (assuming, if you are driving, that you do this safely) and observe the scenery around you. Even though it may be the same drive, train ride, or bus ride that you take every day, there will always be subtle changes taking place. Every day, the seasons will be changing, people will be moving, and nature will be growing. Try to find these subtle differences.

After you arrive at your destination and you are beginning your workday, you may have yet another opportunity to practice your spirituality. Before actually starting your workday, you can take a few moments to be thankful for the work or social experience you are about to embark upon.

170

You could also take a moment to commit to your work in such a way that your work and your interactions can become aligned with your spiritual values. An act such as lighting a candle or having a small sacred object at work (even if it's only a special stone or amulet) can help to remind you of your commitment to your values. Working, playing, and interacting with others can be challenging if those others do not share your values. We cannot always choose with whom we must interact, which requires us to find ways to work positively with them.

If you can approach times of friction and conflict as challenging opportunities for spiritual growth, you can more easily overcome those difficulties. Each conflict can help you practice patience, tolerance, and respect, even in situations in which those things are not being offered to you. For me, my morning meditation practice helps me find a place of deep peace and assurance within myself. I can go to this place even in the face of adversity if I concentrate upon those things. Before work, play, or other group situations, I take a moment to remind myself of that place through a kind of short meditation.

In the midst of the workday, you are offered opportunities to practice other things related to your Pagan spiritual values. At work and in other social situations, you can practice honest communication as you focus on being as authentic as possible. Look for opportunities to offer praise and thanks. Bless others—either silently or aloud—and be willing and grateful to accept the praise and blessings of other people. Remind yourself about your ethical principles and determine how they will affect your interactions with others. Practice empathy and compassion in dealing with others. Listen and be with people. Hopefully, not all your interactions with people at work will be difficult. Also, look for opportunities to offer and share moments of joy. Those moments are equally as important as the other practices you may do at work. It will be those moments that will define your sense of fellowship and camaraderie.

Exercise 2: The Morning

Consider your answers to the following questions. I've provided space here for your answers, or you can write them in your journal or some other study guide.

1. Which of your spiritual goals can best be done in the morning?

_____

_____

_____

_____

_____

_____

2. How will you practice these goals?

_____

_____

_____

_____

_____

_____

The Afternoon

Event	Goal	Practice
Lunch	Honoring Gaia	Blessing the meal
At work (or gathering)	(several)	Continuing work for practices or gatherings
Mid-afternoon	Honoring yourself	Taking a short spiritual break
Going home	Honoring Gaia	Observing beauty

The mid-day meal is another time to be thankful of the blessings of food from Gaia, to enjoy the pleasures of eating, and to find a few moments for yourself. As the workday moves on past lunch, you can continue to work on interaction practices. Keep in mind, however, that most people tend to get tired in the afternoon. I think the idea of an afternoon siesta may be based on great wisdom. Our natural body rhythms tend to dip in the middle of the afternoon. During these times, tensions may rise as fatigue sets in. Most employers, unfortunately, think that the more hours you make a person work, the more he or she will get done. This is simply not so. The more intensely a person concentrates upon a task, the more will be done, but humans tend to be able to focus their concentration intensely only for a short time, after which they need a break. If we scheduled more breaks between intense sessions of application, more work would probably get done, and the health and happiness of the employees would also be promoted. If it is at all possible for you, I suggest that you find a way to take a short spiritual break in the afternoon. This break could be anywhere between a few minutes or a quarter of an hour. During this time, consider doing some basic exercise, such as walking. Take some time to reconnect to Gaia or do a short meditation. Whatever your activity, leave the office or place of work for a few minutes and let yourself clear your head. Later, as you head home from work, you can practice some of the same things you did when you went to work.

Exercise 3: The Afternoon

Consider your answers to the following questions. I've provided space here for your answers, or you can write them in your journal or some other study guide.

1. Which of your spiritual goals can best be done in the afternoon?

_____

_____

_____

_____

_____

2. How will you practice these goals?

_____

_____

_____

_____

_____

The Dusk

Event	Goal	Practice
Dinner	Honoring Gaia	Blessing the meal
After dinner	Honoring Gaia/ Physical Expression	Taking a walk
In social groups	(several)	(same as practices for work)
Evening	Soulful Enveloping/ Honoring yourself	Quiet time or meditation
Before bed	Honoring yourself	Reflecting on good works and joys
Before bed	Soulful Enveloping	Preparing for dreamwork and sleep

Dinner is yet another chance to be thankful for a meal and a chance to gather together with loved ones. Too many times, meals are seen as an inconvenience—something that gets in the way of a busy life. This is unfortunate, because dinner is the one meal when we should be able to truly come together to share ourselves and practice our spirituality. After dinner, consider taking another walk in nature, if possible. It's a great way to aid digestion, connect with Gaia, control weight, and find some quiet time for yourself or with a walking partner. Having an active dog is one way I am assured of taking a lot of walks. If walking alone seems too much of a chore to you, then consider finding a walking partner.

After dinner, people sometimes head to yet another social engagement, such as a class, a meeting, a spiritual group, or an evening out with friends. During work, you took opportunities in your dealings with other people to practice your spiritual principles. At work, however, you usually cannot choose the people with whom you must interact. Your own time is different. You can choose with whom you will spend time. Still, those interactions are times to put values into practice. Being attentive, listening, and offering blessings are just a few of the things that you can do while sharing time with people you enjoy.

As you prepare for bed, there are still more things that you can do as part of your Pagan spiritual practice. Take some quiet time to think about all the blessings and joys of the day. If you did not have any, try to concentrate on how you can find those things in the next day. If you have been able to live up to your values in any small way at any time during the day, then honor yourself with well-deserved praise. Focus on the things you did well rather than those things you felt were not done as well as you had hoped. Visualize how you might have done things differently to be more in line with your values. Think back on all the blessings given to you by Gaia, Spirit, or others. As you climb into bed, prepare yourself for your dreamwork and take a moment to be thankful for the chance to rest. Then, let your body completely relax. Give yourself to Spirit and let your soul dance among the stars.

Exercise 4: The Dusk

Consider your answers to the following questions. I've provided space for your answers, or you can write them in your journal or some other study guide.

1. Which of your spiritual goals can best be done in the dusk of the day?

   _____

   _____

   _____

   _____

   _____

2. How will you practice these goals?

   _____

   _____

   _____

   _____

   _____

Moon Cycles and Developing the Self

With moon cycles, you can begin to work on your goals for developing the self. Each day of the week can have special significance in relation to your practice. The full moon or Esbat ceremony is a good time to work on transforming yourself into the kind of person and Pagan practitioner you want to be. With the dark moon or Astor ceremony, you can meditate on and look toward what you will need to do for the coming Esbat. Esbats and Astors will add special days to your practice with a focus on transforming yourself. That makes them truly magickal.

The Week

Day of the Week	Goal	Practices
Sunday	Soulful Expression	Assessing values Seeking fun
Monday	Emotional Enveloping Emotional Expression	Visiting friends Letting out your feelings
Tuesday	Physical Expression	Sports Sensual activities
Wednesday	Mental Enveloping	Spiritual learning Taking classes
Thursday	Mental Expression	Communicating Teaching
Friday	Emotional Enveloping	Maintaining relationships Social gatherings
Saturday	Balance	Seeking rest Meditation

You can add to your practice some things that you feel need to be done only once a week. For example, we have already looked at the importance of Sunday night, when the day of the sun merges into the day of the moon. Sunday nights are a good time for spiritual reflection and a review of your values and goals. It is also a day to try to have some fun as well. Monday, the day of the moon, is a good day for being with others you love and for revealing your inner hopes and desires. Tuesday, the day of Mars, is a day for letting out that inner energy through sports or exercise. It is also a day for engaging the senses. Wednesday is Mercury's day, and calls us to consider carefully our words, travels, and interactions with others. Thursday is the day of Jupiter, the god of spiritual growth, expansion, and awareness. Venus rules Friday, making it a good day for having fun in social groups and for maintaining relationships, especially romantic ones. Saturday is Saturn's day. As the god of limitations, Saturn calls out to us on that day to accept our own limitations and find rest and renewal. It is the day for seeking balance.

Exercise 5: The Week

Consider your answers to the following questions. I've provided space here for your answers, or you can write them in your journal or some other study guide.

1. Which of your spiritual goals should be done once a week?

_____

_____

_____

_____

_____

2. How will you practice these goals?

_____

_____

_____

_____

_____

The Month

EVENT	GOAL	PRACTICE
Astor	Honoring Gaia/Spirit Developing the self	Ritual to honor the Child Preparation for Esbat activity
Esbat	Honoring Gaia/Spirit Developing the self	Ritual to honor the Goddess Special Esbat activity

The cycle of months is the domain of the moon. Each month contains at least one full and dark moon. With each Astor, Esbat, Sabbat, birthday, and anniversary, you can do the same ritual each time, or you can add a special significance by using any of the techniques discussed in the previous chapter. For example, the Astor is used to celebrate the Divine Child. A ritual for this purpose can be done for every Astor throughout the year. The same can be true for every Esbat ceremony celebrating the Goddess. To add new meaning for each one, however, the Astor and Esbat can also be given special significance according to one of the methods discussed in Chapter 3. For example, you could attach special significance to the full moon according to the Zodiac sign in which the full moon will arise. This adds more work to your overall practice but helps to provide deeper meaning and more of a sense of magick into your spiritual experience. We will use this system as an example of creating special significance to the full moons. Observe the chart shown on page 181.

Sign	Significance	Possible Activity
Aries	Expressive energy for the heart	Tell someone or display your feelings
Taurus	Balanced energy for the body	Seek rest or rejuvenation for the body
Gemini	Enfolding energy for the mind	Seek harmony
Cancer	Expressive energy for the soul	Seek harmony
Leo	Balanced energy for the heart	Still your anger about others and find peace in your heart
Virgo	Enfolding energy for the body	Go to an arts event to seek beauty
Libra	Expressive energy for the mind	Practice compassionate truth
Scorpio	Balanced energy for the soul	Practice non-judgment
Sagittarius	Enfolding energy for the heart	Listen to the feelings of another person
Capricorn	Expressive energy for the body	Partake in movement or exercise for the body
Aquarius	Balanced energy for the mind	Quiet the mind
Pisces	Enfolding energy for the soul	Practice divination

In the previous chart, the Zodiac sign listed is the one in which the next full moon will arise. The use of an astrological calendar will help you determine in which sign each moon will arise. The second column lists the significance according to that sign's related element and virtue (see Chapter 3). During the waxing moon, you would decide what would be the most appropriate activity for self-development based on the significance of that moon. Chapter 2 listed many possibilities, but, through meditation and reflection, you could come up with your own interpretation. When the full moon arrives, you would then begin to work on your selected activity. The third column lists a possible activity to help give you some ideas.

Exercise 6: The Month

Consider your answers to the following questions. I've provided space here for your answers, or you can write them in your journal or some other study guide.

1. Which of your spiritual goals can be done through the celebration of the Esbats and Astors?

_____

_____

_____

_____

_____

_____

2. How will you practice these goals?

_____

_____

_____

_____

_____

Sun Cycles and Helping Others
The Year

The year is the domain of the sun, which determines the cycles of seasons. Pagans honor the changes of the seasons through celebrating Sabbats.

Event	Goal	Practice
Sabbat	Honoring Gaia/Spirit Helping others	Ritual to honor the season Special project for helping others

Sabbats are yet another opportunity to add days of special significance to your practice. Sabbats have traditionally been times when large groups of people come together to celebrate the changes of the seasons. Pagans honor and worship the solstices and equinoxes and those days between by recognizing what each of these changes means for us as a community. Besides being joyous celebrations of the season, Sabbats can also be a chance for the spiritual community to help others.

One way in which the Pagan community can help people in its own area and beyond is to use the celebration of the Sabbat to organize and enact works of charity. As people gather together to honor the seasonal changes, they can also bring forth needed items and organize ways to distribute these items. As do the changes in moon cycles, sun cycles mark different times of the year that can be observed and used. The waxing sun is a good time for bringing things into being, and the waning sun is a good time to clear things away. During the increasing light of the waxing sun, we can work to collect those things that are needed by others to survive and thrive in our society, and we can use the diminishing light of the waning sun to help get these things out to people who need them. Our culture of constant want and desire tends to marginalize and ignore those who are unable to get what they need on their own. Without the help of caring communities, such as the many groups of Pagans around the world, these disconnected people experience untold years of unnecessary suffering and hardship. The sad truth is that if each and every one of us shared a small part of what we had, there would be no homelessness and poverty, but the basis of a capitalistic system such as ours is that its members must constantly buy and not share.

Each Sabbat can become a time for us to realize these things and make a small difference toward changing them or helping those who have been left behind. Through the Sabbats of the waxing sun, we can sow seeds of change and opportunity, and the Sabbats of the waning sun can be a time to harvest those seeds and give out the bounties of goods we have grown and collected. The seeds of sowing can be things such as money and time that are spent to help develop and increase opportunities for growth and sharing. The harvest can be done by collecting those things in which we have invested time and money, and then offering them to those who need them most. The following chart offers some possibilities for offering aid through the Sabbats.

Sabbat	Significance	Possible Activity
Yule	The sowing of the body	Distribute clothing and shelter items A time for healing
Imbolc	The sowing of the heart	Distribute food A time for caring
Ostara	The sowing of the mind	Distribute books A time for learning
Beltane	The sowing of the soul	Distribute spiritual materials A time for listening
Litha	The harvest of the heart	Collect food
Lammas	The harvest of the body	Collect clothing or shelter items
Mabon	The harvest of the soul	Collect spiritual materials
Samhain	The harvest of the mind	Collect books

In this chart, the column on the left lists one of the eight Sabbats. The central column lists the significance of each Sabbat by its appearance on the waning or waxing cycle of the sun and its relationship to the elements.

The third column offers some suggestions for activities. Before celebrating or planning a Sabbat, take some time to determine what activity could be appropriate and useful for helping others based on that Sabbat's significance. During that Sabbat, make plans for engaging in that activity. Based on the wheel of Sabbats, this method offers a way to help the greater community through the four elements and parts of the self, and divides the eight Sabbats by those that appear during the waning and the waxing sun cycles. As an example, during Lammas, as the sun is waxing, clothing can be collected and stored. At Yule, as the sun is waning, efforts can be coordinated to distribute those clothes and to begin setting in place the conditions and efforts needed to encourage another collection at the next Lammas Sabbat. Each Pagan community or practitioner, of course, must consider which needs and methods of offering aid are best and most suited to that community or person.

Exercise 7: The Year

Consider your answers to the following questions. I've provided space here for your answers, or you can write them in your journal or some other study guide.

1. Which of your spiritual goals can be done through the celebration of different Sabbats?

   _____

   _____

   _____

   _____

   _____

2. How will you practice these goals?

_____

_____

_____

_____

_____

The Septenary

In the final chapter of my book *Self-Initiation for the Solitary Witch*, I introduced a 10-year system of growth that used planetary yearly themes combined with moon cycles. I named the system *solunations*. In this section, I will re-introduce the system, but will only concentrate on the seven original "planets" for a seven-year system called a *septenary*.

The septenary, or seven-year cycle, can provide a unique opportunity for a complex yet deeply meaningful practice that combines solar and lunar cycles. Because this is a bit more complex system of extended practice, I do not recommend it for everyone, and you should consider carefully whether or not you wish to include it in your practice. People studying with the Sacred Order of Living Paganism must consider a practice similar to this one in order to complete the final degree. To use this system, you will need to determine the significance of the seven planets to create a theme for each year (see Chapter 3). Once you establish a theme for the year, you will enact this process by determining the significance of the next full moon. For the Astor of the preceding Esbat, you will meditate and reflect upon the focus of the approaching full moon, depending on its assigned meaning, and come up with a spiritual activity that reflects the meaning of the moon and the planet of that year. There are several methods that can be used to create a particular meaning for each Esbat, and my previous book listed quite a few. They include the named-moon method and the astrological method (both discussed in this chapter), the tarot card method, the rune stone method, the chakra method, the elements and deities method (a version of this is used with the astrological method introduced here), and the mythological method. To use any of these systems or another of your choosing, you will simply determine a significance to each element of your system and assign it to each full moon. By combining the meaning of the year with the meaning of the full moon, you will create a complete septenary system.

Through this seven-year system, you will create a powerful set of practices that will focus upon all the major influences and parts of your life. It is especially important to take note of any blocks that arise during this process. If you find yourself unable or unwilling to complete a particular practice based on the focus described in the system, it may be because there is something deeply troubling you about that focus. Through the practice of this septenary, these types of personal challenges are likely to be revealed. Use these opportunities for self-healing and development by not ignoring these difficulties. Reflect on their meaning and discover ways to resolve them. Through this practice, you will gain deep insight into yourself and the world around you.

Exercise 8: The Septenary

Consider your answers to the following questions. I've provided space for your answers, or you can write them in your journal or some other study guide.

1. Which of your spiritual goals can be done through the septenary?

    _____

    _____

    _____

    _____

2. How will you practice these goals?

    _____

    _____

    _____

    _____

    _____

Life Cycles and Honoring Yourself and Others

Throughout our lives, we experience many changes and transitions. Celebrating these changes helps makes them easier and provides meaning to each stage of life. These changes can be celebrated through birthdays and anniversaries.

Event	Goal	Practice
Birthday or anniversary	Honoring yourself	Celebrate life events
Birthday or anniversary	Honoring others	Celebrate the life events of others

As you progress through the various stages and changes of your life, you can take time to celebrate these events through special rituals on or near your birthday or other significant days. Each of the seven-year cycles of life can be honored with a particularly unique ceremony. The following chart offers some ideas for identifying ceremonies that may help to honor those life changes.

STAGE	SUB-STAGE	AGE	CELEBRATION
Child	Baby	1–6	Naming ritual
Maiden/Suitor	Young child	7–13	First-tooth ritual
	Young adult	21–27	Handfasting ceremony
Mother/Father	Adult	28–34	Wedding/birthing
	Mid-life	35–41	Mid-life ritual
	Menopause	42–48	Life accounting
	The Jubilee	49–55	The Jubilee ceremony
Crone/Sage	Senior	56–62	Croning/Saging ritual
	Retirement	63–69	Retirement party
	The Return	70–	Spirit reckoning
	Death		Memorial service

The Child

Within a few days or weeks after being born, a ceremony can be held for parents and the child in which the child is formally named and presented to the world. This is called a Naming ceremony, and recognizes the achievement of the parents as well as the health and well-being of a new child. Many people wait a few days after the actual birth in order to allow both mother and child to gain some strength and to allow the parents to carefully consider a good name. When ready, the parents and their spiritual community gather to present the child with his or her new name. In effect, the new child is being presented to the world and is given his or her first important gift: a name.

As babies grow, their bodies go through many changes. They develop new teeth and go through the painful process of teething. At the next stage of life, babies lose those small baby teeth and begin to grow in their permanent set. This marks an important stage of growth—when the baby develops into a child. The first tooth to be released by the body can become a part of an important ceremony of growth. For most children, the story of the tooth fairy is reenacted during the night of the first and subsequent loss of teeth. Although fun and exciting for children, that particular activity is devoid of any real significance and becomes, rather, a chance to simply get some free money. This event could become even more significant by making it a part of a Pagan ritual in which the first tooth is offered to the Goddess, ritually blessed, wrapped in silk, and placed in the center of the altar. The next morning, the child could unwrap the cloth and find money, treats, or gifts in place of the tooth. Instead of offering the tooth to some unknown tooth fairy who appears only once in life, the tooth could be offered to Gaia or some other deity as a way of learning to value the self and the body, and to learn the lesson about returning to Gaia.

Exercise 9: The Child

Consider your answers to the following questions. I've provided space here for your answers, or you can write them in your journal or some other study guide.

1. How shall you celebrate the life cycles of the Child through your birthday?

_____

_____

_____

2. How can you help others celebrate their life cycles of the Child?

_____

_____

_____

The Maiden/Suitor

At around 14, a child enters into the stage of early adulthood. This is the age when a child can be given an Adulthood or Coming of Age ceremony to recognize the transition from child to maiden or suitor, and to recognize the fact that the body is being prepared to produce children. An Adulthood ceremony should impress upon the young child the awesome consequences and responsibilities that come with sex and pregnancy. Too often, our society ignores this important time of life; this fact makes children feel disoriented. They know that their bodies and minds are going through tremendous changes. Without a ritual to recognize and honor these changes, they possess no meaning. By recognizing these changes, we let children know that they are a normal part of growing up and becoming an adult. As an emerging young person, the child must be willing to balance the freedom of adulthood with the burden of becoming a responsible member of society. Instead of having these changes ignored, they become highlighted, and the children going through them get the support and guidance they need to get through this very trying time. This Adulthood ceremony is actually one of three major Coming of Age rituals included here.

As the capacity to become sexual beings develops, it is only natural for young adults to begin to search for a mate. In our society, this is often done through dating. Unfortunately, the next step in the process of establishing a mate is to go from dating to a permanent commitment of marriage. As we all know, many married couples end up in divorce sometimes after only a few years. Recently, people have taken an intermediate step by first living together with a potential mate before (or instead of) getting married. Usually, though, the act of living together does not include any type of formal commitment to the relationship. This may be fine for some, but others may seek a ceremony that recognizes a commitment in a romantic relationship. For Pagans, there is such a ceremony, and it is called a *Handfasting*. The Handfasting is a ceremony of commitment to a partner in which at least two people promise to stay with each other for a set amount of time—usually a year and a day. I recommend to those considering entering into a long-term relationship with another person that they consider Handfasting before a permanent commitment such as marriage. If the commitment does not work out, then the two can go their separate ways at the end of the agreed time or they can participate in a Handparting ceremony. A Handfasting can also be a permanent commitment if that is what both people agree upon.

Exercise 10: The Maiden/Suitor

Consider your answers to the following questions. I've provided space here for your answers, or you can write them in your journal or some other study guide.

1. How shall you celebrate the life cycles of the Maiden/Suitor through your birthday?

    _____

    _____

    _____

    _____

2. How can you help others celebrate their life cycles of the Maiden/Suitor?

    _____

    _____

    _____

    _____

The Mother/Father

The difference between dating and living together can be great; people often find that relationships change when people share the same living space. It may take several Handfastings or just one before two people find lifetime partners. When they do finally meet each other, they may want to make a permanent commitment, such as through the act of a legal marriage. One primary reason that many people do choose a more lasting commitment is so that they can establish a home and raise children. If the couple decides to have or raise a child, then there will come an opportunity to have a Birthing and Naming ceremony for that new child, whose Wheel of Life will be just beginning.

At some point around the age of 42, women enter the stage of their lives when their bodies no longer can produce children, a stage called *menopause*, or the end of menses. For some women, this can be a time of confusion and sadness. Men, too, can experience this time as one of great frustration, as they begin to feel that their days of youthful vigor and sexual activity are waning. Again, our society does little to recognize this stage of life and help people through it. We can honor this time and support people through its changes with a Mid-life ceremony. Because, for women, this is the second time that a major bodily change takes place, I think it is a good time for a second Coming of Age ceremony. This time, however, the ceremony should represent the newfound freedom and creativity that are available to the person who is now released of the possibility and responsibility of childbirth. For men and women, it can be a chance to honor the need to have one more flight of fancy and fun before really settling in to the waning years of life. Could this be a chance for a second bachelor or bachelorette party? A committed couple would have to discuss their level of comfort with such an idea, but a party may be less expensive than the cost of a new little red sports car, or may be less emotionally damaging than a sexual affair at the office.

At the age of 50, it is time for the grand Jubilee. On your 50th birthday, consider having a grand party celebrating a half-century of existence on this planet. You could have your own Jubilee, and it should be a time so merry that you forgive your hurts to others and ask for forgiveness for those whom you may have hurt. You could ask all the people you have ever known to join your party and make it the celebration of a lifetime.

Let the Jubilee be a time to truly honor all the great things you have done through your life and to celebrate with all the people whose lives you have touched.

Exercise 11: The Mother/Father

Consider your answers to the following questions. I've provided space here for your answers, or you can write them in your journal or some other study guide.

1. How shall you celebrate the life cycles of the Mother/Father through your birthday?

    _____

    _____

    _____

    _____

2. How can you help others celebrate their life cycles of the Mother/ Father?

    _____

    _____

    _____

    _____

The Crone/Sage

At around the age of 56, we reach a stage of life where we can recognize the great experience we have gained in living this life, and we can learn how to begin to pass that learning off to others through wisdom.

This austere time of life is often celebrated in Pagan circles with a ritual of Croning/Saging, in which the elderly person is recognized for his or her contributions to the community and to society. The Croning ceremony is the third of the three Coming of Age rituals.

The next stage is the time in life when most people retire. This is a chance to celebrate one's accomplishments at work and to honor the change from work life to, hopefully, a life of leisure. There was a time when people spent years at the same job and then were treated to a great retirement party complete with gifts and well-wishes from coworkers. Now, people are often forced to move from job to job so that this type of camaraderie does not always exist at the workplace. I hope you will still take the chance when you retire to throw yourself a great party and consider the many great accomplishments you have had in your work life.

There is yet one more stage of the elderly life that may be a bit more somber. This is the time when you have to consider your own mortality. If you have not done so by now, you will need to get your estate in order and prepare for how you will leave this life and what you will provide to others when you are gone. This is also the time to consider what death really means to you. We can do this through a ritual I call the *Spirit Reckoning.* In this ceremony, we consider the meaning of death in order to over come the fear of its impending arrival. We take a chance to reckon with Spirit and put our mind, body, heart, and soul in order so that we can accept death with pride and dignity. Our culture shuns the very thought of death and dying because of our great fear of the ultimate unknown, but Pagans know that death is a part of the great cycle of life. At death we return our souls to that wonderful source of beauty, truth, right, and good of Spirit. We become part of the whole of the universe and a part of all life that will come after our bodies disintegrate and return to our mother Gaia. Though a beautiful thing, it is still frightening to consider the great changes that death brings. Through the ceremony of the Spirit Reckoning, we can come to terms with this awesome truth of existence.

When that final stage of life does come, there will be one more ceremony: the funeral or memorial. Though you obviously cannot take part in that ceremony yourself, you can make plans to let others know how you wish to be remembered. Take some time in your life to decide how you wish your body to be treated and what kind of ceremony would honor you and your spiritual values. Make sure others know this information and talk to them about it. This is very important not only to you, but to those who will want to honor you.

Exercise 12: The Crone/Sage

Consider your answers to the following questions. I've provided space here for your answers, or you can write them in your journal or some other study guide.

1. How shall you celebrate the life cycles of the Crone/Sage through your birthday?

_____

_____

_____

_____

_____

_____

2. How can you help others celebrate their life cycles of the Crone/ Sage?

_____

_____

_____

_____

_____

Putting It All Together
Steps for Incorporation

Now that you have observed how spiritual goals can be combined with the many sacred cycles of the universe, it is time to develop your own practice. To do that, you will need a plan of action. Here it is:

1. Create a chart of goals.
2. Determine the cycles to follow.
3. Create a coordinated chart of goals and cycles.
4. Add these practices slowly into your life.

Begin by reviewing the answers to the exercises in Chapter 2, and create a chart of your goals. Make sure the chart is balanced in terms of the types of activities: whether they include all the elements and whether or not the activity will be fun or work for you. Then determine how often each activity should be performed: daily, weekly, monthly, or yearly. Also include a plan for special days, such as for each Esbat, Astor, and Sabbat. Next, determine which cycles you will follow. A complete plan will include activities for each of the four parts of the day, activities to be done once a week, and special activities for the Esbats, Astors, and Sabbats. You should also decide if you wish to practice the septenary. You may not want to include all of these at first, and we will discuss a plan to help you institute them slowly, if needed. The third step is to create a coordinated chart that connects your activities to the cycles in which they are most appropriate. When you have completed this, you may want to create or mark a calendar with things to help remind you of your goals or you may create your own special calendar. Be sure to include special days such as those of the full moons, dark moons, Sabbats, birthdays, and special anniversaries.

Year	Related Cycle	Subset	Practices
1	Gaia cycles	The day	Regular practices for the day
2	Moon cycles	The week	Regular practices for the week
3	Moon cycles	The month	Regular practices for Esbats and Astors
4	Moon cycles	The month	Special practices for Esbats and Astors
5	Sun cycles	The year	Regular practices for Sabbats
6	Sun cycles	The year	Special practices for Sabbats
7	Life cycles	The septenary	Special practices for seven-year cycles and birthdays

There is another system for slowly adding these things into your life. In fact, it is another version of the septenary. Through it, you can add one type of cycle per year for seven years until you have begun to work in a complete system. This is a great way for the beginning solitary practitioner who needs to more slowly incorporate many of these things.

With this method, you can take a long time to coordinate and add practices to your overall system until you reach your final goal. In the first year, develop regular practices for the day that honor Gaia and Spirit. In the second year, add practices that relate to particular days of the week. In the third year, you can begin to celebrate regular Esbats and Astors by celebrating the Goddess at the Esbat and the Child at the Astor. The fourth year can be used to add the special practices of each Esbat and Astor to reach your goals of developing the self. In the fifth year, you can develop your standard Sabbat rituals, and the next year can be used to add the special practices to each Sabbat designed to aid others. The seventh year can be used to add special practices for honoring the self and others through special birthday and anniversary celebrations or by adding the septenary practice discussed earlier.

Things to Keep in Mind

In putting together your Pagan practice, here are some other things to keep in mind.

1. Be consistent.

2. Be flexible.

3. Make sure your practices reflect your values.

Be consistent. Establish a practice and stick with it for at least six months. There is a certain novelty in trying out something new. It can be fun and exciting at first, but the excitement will wear off after a few months of practice. In order for any spiritual practice to have a lasting effect, the practitioner must be willing to stick with it. Spirituality cannot be a passing fad, but must be a sincere practice.

Be flexible. Although consistency is important, there must also be some room for flexibility. There will come unavoidable circumstances that will demand some change in your practice, even if only temporarily. Decide if these circumstances are due to forces beyond your control or if they appear because of your own resistance to change. Boredom can become an excuse to not see something through—especially if that something involves needed changes within yourself. If a change is necessary because natural circumstances change, then be flexible. If excuses come through because of fear or a lack of commitment, be consistent.

Make sure your practices reflect your Pagan values. Always consider whether or not what you are doing truly reflects the values and goals that you established in the first chapter. Sometimes a practice can begin to take on other values, such as self-adoration or worship. Are you doing these things to brag about your moral superiority to others? Does doing these things make you feel as if you are a greater person than others? Do you do these things to impress or shock your students, your friends, your parents, or others? If you answer yes to any of these things, then you are practicing for the wrong reasons. Consider looking again at the reasons at the beginning of this book. This is also the reason for doing a weekly values check-in with yourself. Just as a runner checks his pulse during a race to monitor his health, you should also check your reasons and motivations for your Pagan spiritual practice. Review your reasons for starting this practice. Review your Pagan values. Then see if your practice continues to reflect these things.

5

Rituals for
Celebrating the Cycles

Introduction

In this chapter I will offer some suggestions for designing some simple rituals to help you celebrate and practice many of the things discussed in this text. I have not provided complete rituals here. There are many sources for that: books, the Internet, and local circles all have plenty of ritual resources. What I have done is to simply provide you with a framework from which to begin creating your own rituals. You can use the format of this framework to help you design other rituals not included here as well. Feel free to use what you need and alter the ideas as you need to make your own meaningful rituals.

These rituals are designed primarily for solitary practitioners but could be easily adopted for group use. Most groups, covens, or circles already have quite a few rituals, but people practicing on their own might not. The ideas listed here could provide a basis for stand-alone rituals, or they could be part of a larger ritual procedure. Some basic elements of a standard Pagan ritual are listed in the next section. These rituals are also meant to be simple and short. For those who have little time to do a long ceremony, short rituals are ideal. To make these into longer ceremonies, simply add on more ritual procedures as you see fit. If you are a solitary practitioner, I recommend that you develop your own personal ritual procedure and follow it closely for each ritual. Again, there are many great texts that describe how you can do this. However, I want to mention some of the things that are important to a Pagan ritual so that you may add them into your own ritual process if you so desire.

The Elements of a Pagan Ritual

The Pagan ritual is designed to reflect and honor the cycles of the universe because it, too, is a cycle in itself. A ritual begins in darkness similar to the dark moon, increase in light and energy similar to the waxing moon, rise to a full height of light and activity similar to the full moon, and then decrease in light and energy similar to the waning moon until they once again return to the darkness similar to the dark moon. The fact that all Pagan rituals are done within circles also reflects their cyclic nature and their worship of those sacred cycles of life. We recognize that, just as the moon does not possess its own light but reflects the light of the sun, our Pagan rituals are not energized by ourselves but rather derive their power and energy from Spirit, and we are a reflection of that source of all energy. Therefore, a ritual has five main parts: the preparation or darkness, the beginning or waxing phase, the middle or full phase, the ending or waning phase, and then the return to the darkness. Each of these five sections has parts of a full ritual that help to bring in the light and energy to the circle, depending on the focus of the ceremony. Here is the entire list of sections within a typical Pagan ritual:

▷ Darkness.

- Silence and concentration.

▷ Waxing.

- State intention.

- Sanctify the space.

- Cast the circle.

- Center yourself.

- Set the four quadrants.

- Call the deities.

- Raise energy.

▷ Full.

- Ritual work based on the intent of the ritual.

▷ Waning.

- Release deities.

- Release quadrants.

- Open the circle.

- End.

▷ Darkness.

- Ground.

Before beginning a ritual, I suggest you take some time to carefully review what you want to do and then make sure that you have assembled all your materials. After having created a ritual circle, nothing destroys the magick of the moment faster than having to run out of the room to find the lighter you forgot.

After preparing your space and yourself, I suggest you begin in relative darkness, if possible. The darkness, of course, can be symbolic instead of literal and may be necessarily so if you are doing a small ritual in your office during the middle of the day. In true darkness, we often can find peace and a sense of reverence, or we may find a sense of fear of the unknown. Try to find an appreciation of the darkness (one reason for celebrating Astors) as a part of the great cycles of light and dark. Darkness is not to be feared, but to be respected and honored, for without darkness there would be no appreciation of the light. Once you have learned to respect the dark, establish that sense of respect and worship as the state of mind needed to begin a ritual.

In the waxing part of the ritual procedure, you slowly begin to add light and energy to the ceremony. Begin by stating your intention and lighting a candle. All rituals should begin with a clear statement of what the ceremony is meant to honor. I call the candle lit with intent the "working candle." It is the first candle to be lit, it is the candle that shall light all others, and it is the last candle to be extinguished. In a simple ritual, a working candle may be all that is needed. Next, sanctify your space as a sacred place in which to work. Cast a real or drawn circle around you and all the objects and space in which you are working. Take a few minutes to center yourself so that you may focus on your goal. Next, set the four quadrants (some call them the "watchtowers"). They usually represent the four compass directions and the four elements of Earth, Air, Fire, and Water. The traditional manner of calling the quadrants is to begin in the North (or East) and move clockwise around the circle. Then the particular deities sacred to the practitioner are called. In some circles, a generic title of God and Goddess and Child are called. With each of the quadrants and deities, candles are lit so that light is increased in the circle. The final part of the waxing phase of the ritual is the raising of energy.

When the waxing phase has been completed, and the light and energy of the circle have been raised, it is time for the actual ritual work itself. As with the nights of the full moon, this is the time for magick. Your ritual work will be based upon whatever goals and intent you set for the ritual itself. The ritual ideas given in this chapter will be ways that you can create the work that would be done at this part of the ritual process.

When the ritual work is done, it is time for the waning phase of the ceremony. In this section, the light and energy are allowed to dissipate as you return to the mundane world just beyond the circle. You should release the light and energy in the exact opposite order in which they were first done. Begin by releasing whatever deities you invoked. Remember, though, that these are deities you have called; they are not house servants. You do not just tell them to go away. Ask them kindly to return from whence they came and heartily thank them for their participation. Extinguish the candles you set for them. Next, release the four quadrants you set, but in the opposite direction. Begin in the North (or East) and move counterclockwise, extinguishing the candles in each direction. Finally, end your ritual by opening the circle you created around you and finish up. The very last step should be an announcement that the ritual has ended. The working candle is extinguished, leaving you in the relative literal or figurative darkness where you began.

The return to darkness should call you to drain all excess energy and reflect upon what you have done. Releasing any excess energy raised is done through a process called *grounding*, which involves returning your energy to Gaia. The easiest way to do this is to let yourself touch Gaia and feel energy draining into her, much as a grounding rod does with electricity. After grounding, give yourself a few moments in the silence to appreciate the sense of peace that comes over you and to reflect on what has been done.

The Format for Ritual Work

The rituals given in this chapter include several similar elements. Each one will include a ritual name to identify its purpose, a best time for doing the ritual, some general goals and some specific goals for the ceremony, one or more things to bless, items to use, a set of vows, and a short list of possible activities. The rituals will be named in accordance with the spiritual practices discussed in earlier chapters and will be organized by the specific cycles mentioned. In cases where specific times are not suggested through the coordination of goals and cycles, other times will be suggested. Each ritual will include the general goals it can fulfill in relation to the spiritual goals of Chapter 2.

Within the work of most sacred ceremonies is the blessing in which the practitioner asks for certain objects, places, or things to be blessed. How you see this type of blessing actually taking place will depend on your specific Pagan theological perspective. The very act of requesting a blessing means that you recognize that you are not the sole power present in the circle—a greater power is also present. Certainly you are doing the blessing, but you are asking for a special recognition to be added to your object of blessing. Through Spirit, you imbibe special honor and energy into those things that are blessed. Most rituals also include a vow that the participants take in order to dedicate themselves to the purpose of the ceremony. These vows should be very simple yet sincere. Do not take a vow that you have no intention of fulfilling. Do not feel that you need to make a vow unless you really want to and it feels right for you to do so. After the vow, there are often some additional activities that can be added to help you succeed in your goal for the ritual.

The Rituals

Rituals for Gaia Cycles: The Morning

Name of ritual: Waking.

Best time: Mornings.

General goals:
1. Accepting blessings.
2. Honoring yourself.

Specific goals:
1. To rise in a positive attitude.
2. To visualize a good day.
3. To visualize the self as you wish to be seen.

Possible blessings:
1. For a good night's sleep.
2. For waking to a beautiful day.
3. For a time of morning quiet and reflection.

Items to use:
1. White or yellow working candle.

Vows:

    1. To doing your best to be authentic and true to your Pagan values throughout the day.

Activities:

Take a few moments of quiet time to visualize how you can be truly Pagan and true to yourself and your values throughout the day. Actually see yourself in your mind and set yourself in possible situations in which you might find yourself in the upcoming day. Remind yourself of the kind of person you want to be, and be willing to forgive yourself when you do not always meet these standards. Be thankful for the chance to live and practice another day.

• • • • • • •

Name of ritual: Morning Meditation.

Best time: Mornings.

General goals:

    1. Soulful enveloping.

Specific goals:

    1. To find a sense of inner peace.

    2. To connect to Spirit.

    3. To quiet the active mind.

    4. To prepare yourself for the day.

Possible blessings:

    1. For the time to meditate.

    2. For yourself.

    3. For connecting to Spirit.

    4. For the peace of the universe.

Items to use:

1. Purple working candle.

2. An amulet or stone.

Vows:

1. To take this time to quiet the mind.

2. To focus on peace for now and throughout the day.

Activities:

State your intent and light the purple working candle. Sit quietly for at least five minutes (20 would be better) and let your mind and body relax. Focus on the energy of Gaia and sky, or of Spirit entering into you as you breathe, filling you with the great peace of the universe. Let the strength of Gaia and Her infinite patience fill you. Focus on the breath as it moves slowly and fully in and out of your body, filling you with the energies of the gods. Try to carry this peace in your heart throughout the day. Hold a stone or amulet as your meditate and then carry this with you to remind you of the state of mind you were in when you held it.

• • • • • • •

➤ Name of ritual: Beginning Work.

Best time: When you first arrive at work.

General goals:

1. Offering blessings.

2. Honoring others.

Specific goals:

1. To set a positive attitude before starting work.

2. To honor the office in which you work.

3. To honor the other people with whom you will be involved during work.

Possible blessings:
1. Yourself.

2. The office.

3. Coworkers, clients, and supervisors.

Items to use:
1. Blue working candle.

2. Incense or another small object.

Vows:
1. To work with others in a positive frame of mind.

2. To honor yourself and others during work.

3. To do work that is good and for right.

Activities:

Take a few moments before starting work to offer some silent blessings to yourself and to others. Visualize yourself living your Pagan values through your work and relationships. Use a small object, such as a candle, stone, incense, or other object that will represent and remind you of your goals for work. Make sure the object does not offend others at your workplace. For most people that object will have to be something that looks fairly innocent. A small stone, a flower, a small bell, and a nonreligious figurine all look to be simple desk paraphernalia but can have special meaning to you.

• • • • • • •

Rituals for Gaia Cycles: The Afternoon

🐾 Name of ritual: The Afternoon Break.

Best time: Mid-afternoon.

General goals:

1. Honoring yourself.

Specific goals:

1. To take a short spiritual break from work.

2. To quiet the mind.

3. To remind yourself of your goals and values for work.

Possible blessings:

1. For yourself.

2. For your work.

3. For a beautiful day.

Items to use:

1. Same item used at beginning of work.

Vows:

1. To maintain the goals you set before work.

Activities:

Take the object you blessed before work and take a few moments of silence to quiet your mind and take a moment of rest. Remind yourself of your spiritual goals and values you have for work. If you can, take a short walk and get out of the office for a few moments. Take some deep breaths and feel your mind and body relax. Return to work refreshed.

• • • • • • •

Name of ritual: Evening Meditation.

Best time: Evenings.

General goals:

1. Soulful enveloping.

2. Honoring yourself.

Specific goals:

1. To find a sense of inner peace.

2. To connect to Spirit.

3. To quiet the active mind.

4. To prepare yourself for the evening.

Possible blessings:

1. For the time to meditate.

2. For yourself.

3. For connecting to Spirit.

4. For the peace of the universe.

Items to use:

1. Purple working candle.

Vows:

1. To take this time to quiet the mind.

2. To focus on peace for now and throughout the day.

Activities:

State your intent and light the purple working candle. Let your mind and body relax. Concentrate on thoroughly draining and cleansing yourself of all the energies you absorbed and raised during the day. Prepare yourself for the evening's relaxation and rest.

• • • • • • •

Name of ritual: Meal Blessing.

Best time: Before each meal, but especially before the final or largest meal of the day.

General goals:

1. Honoring Gaia and Spirit.

Specific goals:

1. To honor Gaia and Spirit for the gifts of food you have been given.

2. To honor those who have helped bring you this food.

3. To focus on the enjoyment of the meal.

4. To celebrate the time to be together with family or friends.

Possible blessings:

1. For the food.

2. For the drink.

3. For those who have cooked and prepared the food.

4. For those who labored to make the food available.

5. For those gathered around to eat.

Items to use:

1. Green working candle or other candles.

2. Glass of water or other liquid.

Vows:

1. To eat with intent.

2. To return the gift of food by doing good works.

Activities:

Offer a blessing either silently or aloud in thanks for the food. Consider the food as a gift from Gaia. Think about eating the food slowly and enjoying it and the company of those gathered with you to eat. You can light a candle or set of candles in honor of your blessing and as a reminder through the meal to eat with intent. One old tradition is to raise a glass of liquid and toast to the gods while spilling a little of the drink on the ground as a sacrifice to Gaia. I modify this a bit by dipping my finger in the water and dripping a few drops on my plate while I offer a blessing and a vow to use the energy obtained from the food to do good works.

• • • • • • •

Name of ritual: Before Bed.

Best time: Before going to sleep.

General goals:

1. Accepting blessings.

2. Honoring yourself.

3. Soulful Enveloping.

Specific goals:

1. To prepare yourself for sleep.

2. To prepare for dreamwork.

3. To take an account of the day.

Possible blessings:

1. For having a good day.

2. For being with others.

3. For being authentic to yourself and others.

4. For succeeding in your spiritual goals.

5. For a good sleep.

6. To help those you met today who are suffering.

7. To ask for aid in your own sufferings.

Items to use:
1. Black working candle.

2. Small stone or amulet.

Vows:
1. To be open to intuition found through dreams.

2. To forgive yourself and all others for any wrongful acts.

Activities:

As you prepare for bed, light a candle of intent (but do not fall asleep with it lit). Take a few minutes to recall your day. Think back on all the joys and pleasures of the day, no matter how small or insignificant they may seem. Recall if you were true or not to your Pagan goals. If you were not, do not deride yourself, but simply imagine ways in which you might do better next time. Mostly, forgive yourself and others and focus on the things you did well so that you can amplify them in the future. Extinguish your candle. Hold your amulet in your hands and concentrate on letting yourself be open to dreamwork for the night. Make sure you have a notebook and a pen by your bed to record your dreams in the morning. Place the amulet under your pillow or near your bed to remind yourself of your goal. Let yourself slowly relax until you fall into a peaceful sleep.

Rituals for Moon Cycles: The Week

Name of ritual: A Day of Rest.

Best time: Once a week.

General goals:

1. Honoring yourself.

Specific goals:

1. To find some time at least once a week when you can relax for several hours.

Possible blessings:

1. For a good week.

2. For having a chance to relax.

3. For renewed energy.

Items to use:

1. A special item of clothing.

Vows:

1. To honor yourself through taking a rest or doing something you enjoy.

2. To honor the need for all people to rest.

Activities:

Bless a special item of clothing such as a worn-out baseball hat that, when worn, will indicate to you and others that you are officially "off-duty" for the next couple of hours. During this time of the week you are no longer a person of duty, rank, or title. You shall just be yourself. Allow yourself to become completely self-absorbed in something you really love to do or in just kicking up your feet and resting. You have worked hard all week at being the best worker, spouse, partner, and authentic Pagan you can be. You deserve a rest!

• • • • • • •

⮞ Name of ritual: Weekly Ritual.

Best time: Sunday evenings.

General goals:

1. Soulful expression.

Specific goals:

1. To gather together with other Pagans.

or

2. To review your Pagan values and goals, and assess your progress.

Possible blessings:

1. For others who gather with you.

2. For doing good work toward your spiritual goals.

3. For Spirit and its presence with you in your work.

4. For Gaia for giving you strength in your goals.

Items to use:

1. Orange working candle.

Vows:

1. To continue with your practice.

2. To remain true to your goals.

3. To work to aid yourself and others.

Activities:

Light your candle of intent. Review the goals you set out for yourself and any vows you chose to take. Remind yourself of your reasons for wanting to take on this practice. Take time to contemplate each goal and what it means to you. Contemplate your spiritual values and observe any changes in your thoughts and attitude. Recommit yourself to your goals and to living a Pagan life.

• • • • • • •

Rituals for Moon Cycles: The Month

☞ Name of ritual: The Astor.

Best time: Evenings of the dark moon.

General goals:

1. Honoring Gaia/Spirit.
2. Developing the self.

Specific goals:

1. To honor the stars.
2. To honor the deity of Child.
3. To honor the force of Life or the manifestation of Spirit.
4. To prepare for your special goal for the upcoming Esbat.

Possible blessings:

1. For the stars.
2. For the Child.
3. For all beings.
4. For all life-forms.

Items to use:

1. Purple working candle.

2. Representation of Child deity.

3. Your chart of special Esbat activities.

Vows:

1. To honor all forms of life.

2. To honor Child.

3. To honor androgyny in all forms.

4. To intend to harm none.

5. To work toward your special Esbat goal.

Activities:

Light your candle of intent. If possible, take some time to enjoy the beauty of the starlit night. Reflect on the beauty of all life-forms. Offer blessings to the Child or other deity of life. Look upon the chart of special Esbat activities you have created from Chapter 4 and find the special activity or significance for the next approaching Esbat. Use the next two weeks as time to reflect and meditate on that goal to determine how you will bring it about during the time of the next full moon.

• • • • • • •

Name of ritual: The Esbat.

Best time: Evenings of the full moon.

General goals:

1. Honoring Gaia/Spirit.

2. Developing the self.

Specific goals:

    1. To honor the moon.

    2. To honor the deity of Goddess.

    3. To honor the force of love or the enfolding of Spirit.

    4. To work on developing your spiritual self.

    5. To honor the special significance of this Esbat.

Possible blessings:

    1. For the moon.

    2. For the darkness and coolness of the night.

    3. For the Goddess.

    4. For the gift of love that blesses all life.

    5. For the cycles of the moon.

Items to use:

    1. Green working candle.

    2. Representation of Goddess deity.

    3. Your chart of special Esbat significance and activities.

Vows:

    1. To honor femininity in all forms.

    2. To honor Goddess.

    3. To love yourself and all beings.

Activities:

Light your candle of intent. Offer blessings and respects to the Goddess or another feminine deity. Honor the face of the Goddess. Reflect on the power of love and its effect on the cycles of life. Consider how you can become more loving of yourself and others. Enact your special activity for this Esbat.

• • • • • • •

Rituals for Sun Cycles: The Year

Name of ritual: The Sabbat.

Best time: Solstices, equinoxes, and cross-quarter days.

General goals:

1. Honoring Gaia/Spirit.

2. Helping others.

Specific goals:

1. To honor the sun.

2. To honor the deity of God.

3. To honor the force of light or the expression of Spirit.

4. To prepare for your special Sabbat goal.

5. To honor the special significance of this Sabbat.

6. To help alleviate the suffering of others.

Possible blessings:

1. For the sun.

2. For the light and warmth of the day.

3. For the God.

4. For the strength of light that blesses all life.

5. For the cycles of the sun.

Items to use:

1. Red working candle.

2. Representation of God deity.

3. Your chart of special Sabbat significance and activities.

Vows:

1. To honor masculinity in all forms.

2. To honor God.

3. To respect yourself and all beings.

Activities:

Light your candle of intent. Offer blessings and respects to the God or another masculine deity. Honor the myth of the dying and reborn God. Reflect on the power of light and its effect on the cycles of life. Observe the importance of the particular season and its effects on life. Consider how you can respect and encourage growth in yourself and others. Enact your special activity for this Sabbat.

• • • • • • •

Name of ritual: Birthdays.

Best time: Your birthday and the birthdays of others.

General goals:

1. Honoring yourself and others.

Specific goals:

1. To honor the goods works you have done through the year.

2. To honor the particular stage of your life you are in or entering.

Possible blessings:

1. For yourself for your good works this year.

2. For others who have loved, taught, and blessed you this year.

3. For your deities or Spirit.

Items to use:

    1. Yellow working candle or birthday candles.

    2. Chart of life cycles and significances.

Vows:

    1. To continue to do good works.

    2. To honor and bless those who come into your life.

    3. To respect and honor your family and friends.

Activities:

Light your candle of intent or follow the continuing Pagan tradition of lighting birthday candles. Reflect on your past year. What were your joys and sorrows? How did you live out your Pagan values? How were your relationships with others? Consider how you will live out the next year and how you will continue to strengthen your values and goals. If this is one of the special birthdays of the seven-year life cycles, create and enact a special ritual or celebration based on the theme of that life stage (see the rituals that follow).

• • • • • • •

Rituals for Life Cycles: The Child

Name of ritual: Paganing.

    Best time: Within a few weeks after birth, at the first new moon.

    General goals:

        1. Honoring yourself and others.

    Specific goals:

        1. Honoring the new child.

        2. Honoring the new parents.

3. Celebrating with loved ones.

4. Choosing and announcing name of new child.

5. Announcing and honoring the "godparents."

Possible blessings:

1. The child.

2. The mother.

3. The father.

4. The guardians.

5. The "godparents."

6. Those who are there to support the parents.

7. The gods for the birth of a new child.

8. Gaia for supporting the child.

Items to use:

1. White or working candle.

2. Blessed water.

Vows:

1. To honor, support, and love the child.

2. To support the parents or guardians.

3. To support the "godparents."

Activities:

Light your candle of intent. Bless the new baby by anointing her with sacred water. Present the child to the world and announce his or her new name. Have the parents or guardians vow their love and support to the child. Have the others there vow their support to the parents and the child. Announce and bless the child's "godparents." (Goddess-parents?) You might also decide to vow to raise the child as a Pagan until such time as he or she can choose a sacred path.

· · · · · · ·

Name of ritual: First Tooth.

Best time: Just after a child's first baby tooth falls out, during the waning moon.

General goals:

1. Honoring yourself and others.

Specific goals:

1. To honor this stage of the child's life.

2. To honor the gift of the tooth to the gods.

3. To help introduce a child to her own special ritual.

Possible blessings:

1. For the tooth.

2. For the continued growth of the child.

Items to use:

1. Purple working candle.

2. An altar or sacred space.

3. Silk wrapping.

4. The tooth (cleaned and dried).

Vows:

1. To honor changes and the natural cycles of the body.

2. To protect and love the child through all his or her life changes.

Activities:

Light your candle of intent. Bless the tooth through the four elements. Wrap it in silk and ask that it be protected through the night. Place it in the center of the altar or sacred space and dedicate it as a gift to the gods. Let the child go to bed. Bury the tooth and bless it once more. In place of the tooth, place candy or other small gifts on the altar.

Rituals for Life Cycles: The Maiden/Suitor

Name of ritual: Adulthood (Coming of Age I).

Best time: At around the 14th birthday, at the moon's waxing half.

General goals:

1. Honoring yourself and others.

Specific goals:

1. To honor the entering of a child into adulthood.

2. To teach lessons about sex and responsible sexuality.

3. To honor parents and friends.

Possible blessings:

1. For the child.

2. For the gift of sexuality.

Items to use:

1. Red working candle.

2. Four keys in each of the elemental colors.

3. Large ritual circle.

4. Temporary tattoos.

5. A ritual gate.

6. Food for feasting.

7. Letter and envelope.

Vows:

1. To be a responsible adult.

2. To respect the power of sex.

3. To honor and treat the child as an adult.

Activities:

This is the first of three Coming of Age rituals that celebrate major changes in life. Before the ritual, have the child write a letter to himself or herself expressing hopes and desires for the future. Place this letter in an envelope, seal it (preferably with a wax seal), and place it in a safe place for the future. Create a large ritual working space. Have the child become temporarily tattooed with images that represent adulthood. Light your candle of intent. Have the child pass through the ritual gate and then go around the circle and receive instructions and challenges from each of the four quarters. After each challenge, give the child a key or other symbol of maturity. At each direction, the child should be given lessons about sexuality and the awesome responsibilities that come with it. Parents and others should vow to support and honor the child and promise henceforth to recognize and treat him or her as an adult. The child is then announced to the world as having become a new adult. A celebratory feast should then follow.

• • • • • • •

Name of ritual: Handfasting.

Best time: When deciding to make a temporary or permanent commitment to a relationship, at a full moon.

General goals:
1. Honoring yourself and others.

Specific goals:
1. To honor the new couple.
2. To have the couple make a public announcement of commitment.
3. To instruct the new couple on the responsibilities of commitment.

Possible blessings:
1. For the new couple.
2. For the blossoming of new love.
3. For those who promise to support the couple.

Items to use:
1. A red cord of at least 3 yards in length.
2. Two glasses and a beverage.
3. Ritual besom or broom.
4. Pink working candle; red and green candles.

Vows:
1. To each person in the relationship to honor and support the other.
2. To the couple by others.
3. To have the relationship follow in Pagan ways.
4. To remain committed to each other for the time agreed upon (at least a year and a day).

Activities:

This is one of few rituals in which an officiant is probably necessary. Process the new couple to a ritual circle. Let the male carry the red candle and the female the green candle (adjust according to the sexes of the participants). When they reach the circle, the couple should jointly light the candle of intent but not extinguish their individual candles. Have them state their commitment to each other (include the determined time frame) and state their vows to each other and to the gods. Instruct them on the meaning and responsibilities of a Pagan relationship. Seal the vows of commitment with a toast and a kiss. Ritually tie together (gently, of course) one of each of the hands of the couple with three rings around the hands to represent a commitment to one another, to each other, and to the gods. Present the couple to the participants as a new couple. Have them jump across the broom as they exit the circle.

• • • • • • •

Rituals for Life Cycles: The Mother/Father

 Name of ritual: Wedding.

Best time: When making a permanent commitment to a relationship, during full moon.

General goals:

1. Honoring yourself and others.

Specific goals:

1. To honor the new couple.

2. To have the couple make a public announcement of marriage.

3. To instruct the new couple on the responsibilities of marriage.

Possible blessings:

1. For the new couple.

2. For the blossoming of new love.

3. For those who promise to support the couple.

Items to use:

1. A red cord of at least 3 yards in length.

2. Two glasses and a beverage.

3. Ritual besom or broom.

4. Pink working candle; red and green candles.

5. Rings or other tokens of commitment.

Vows:

1. To each person in the relationship to honor and support the other.

2. To the couple by others.

3. To have the relationship follow in Pagan ways.

4. To remain committed to each other permanently.

Activities:

The differences between a Handfasting and a wedding is that a wedding is a legally binding ceremony requiring an ordained or state recognized officiant, and it requires a permanent commitment to the relationship (rather than a prescribed limit of time). The ceremony should be quite similar to the Handfasting, but should also include tokens of permanent commitment, such as rings or other worn items. Be sure to follow all regulations required by the state in which the ceremony is held.

• • • • • • •

Name of ritual: Mid-life (Coming of Age II).

Best time: At around the 35th birthday; at the dark moon.

General goals:

1. Honoring yourself and others.

Specific goals:

1. To honor life accomplishments.

2. To recognize the spiritual call.

3. To celebrate the fruits of labor.

Possible blessings:

1. For the person in mid-life.

2. For the second half of life.

3. For continued strength, wisdom, love, and peace.

Items to use:

1. Blue working candle.

2. Four fruits in each of the elemental colors (such as banana, apple, blueberries, and green grapes).

3. Large ritual circle.

4. Temporary tattoos.

5. A ritual gate.

6. Food for feasting.

7. The letter written at the first Coming of Age ritual.

8. Letter and envelope.

Vows:

1. To honor the past.

2. To continue to do good works.

Activities:

This is the second of three Coming of Age rituals that mark major milestones in the life of every person. To prepare for this ritual, the initiate should take time to review all past accomplishments. This is also the time in most people's lives when they feel called to a deeper spirituality. Create a large ritual working space. Have the initiate become temporarily tattooed with images that represent mid-life. Light your candle of intent. Have the initiate pass through the ritual gate and then go around the circle and receive instructions and challenges from each of the four quarters. After each challenge, give the initiate a piece of fruit or other symbol of mid-life. Other symbols can include bits of colored yarn to represent the life that has been weaved thus far, colored masks to represent the faces we put on in the different parts of our lives, or small notebooks with colored covers to represent the wisdom that will be written in the years to come. At each direction, the initiate should be given a chance to review accomplishments.

> Earth = work
>
> Air = education and intellectual
>
> Fire = relationships and family
>
> Water = spiritual accomplishments

Others at the ceremony should be given a chance to also recognize good works. At the end of the ceremony, the initiate should open the letter written at the first Coming of Age ritual. This may be read aloud or silently. Another letter should be written and sealed for the future. A feast should follow the ceremony.

• • • • • • •

Name of ritual: Life Accounting.

Best time: At around the 42nd birthday, at the full moon.

General goals:

    1. Honoring yourself and others.

Specific goals:

    1. Honoring the passing of menopause (for women).

    2. Accounting past goals.

    3. Releasing unneeded goals.

    4. Determining future goals and possible legacy.

    5. Counting life's blessings.

Possible blessings:

    1. For the freedom of the end of childbirth years.

    2. For continued health and happiness.

Items to use:

    1. Green working candle.

    2. Writing materials.

Vows:

    1. To continue to look for life's blessings.

Activities:

    In contrast to the previous Mid-life ritual, this ritual is meant to be more somber and private. At some point in every year, a business must take stock of what it has in its inventory so the owners know what they have to sell in the future. In the same sense, we can take this chance to take stock of the blessings we have had in our lives and consider the talents we have developed and can use in our future to determine our place in history. We all have a place in history no matter how small, for each of our lives affects the lives of others. Light your candle of intent. Take some time to consider the blessings you have had in your life. Write them down. Also consider the goals that you have consciously or unconsciously set for yourself. Determine whether these goals are really appropriate for your life. You may need to revise them and make them more realistic, or they may be based on false assumptions of the past. For example, instead of focusing on being rich and famous, you may want to focus your life more on loving and being loved. Consider what you want your legacy in life to be and then make plans to have it happen.

• • • • • • •

Name of ritual: The Jubilee.

Best time: Planning begins at the 49th birthday, and the party at around the 50th birthday, at the full moon.

General goals:

1. Honoring yourself and others.

Specific goals:

1. To celebrate the passing of seven cycles of seven years.

2. To seek and grant forgiveness.

3. To settle all debts and grudges in a positive way.

Possible blessings:

1. For continued health and prosperity.

2. For the person who is celebrating the Jubilee.

3. For all those gathered to celebrate.

Items to use:

1. Silver working candle.
2. Party items.
3. Gifts to the celebrant.
4. Crown.

Vows:

1. To forgive those who may have caused pain.
2. To live so that you shall not need beg forgiveness from others.

Activities:

This should be an all-out fun affair for all involved, but there is quite a bit of serious work and preparation that will need to go into it beforehand. The Jubilee is a celebration of a new start. In order to do that, you will need to look back over your past and offer forgiveness to all those who may have hurt you. This does not mean that you ever need to put yourself in a bad situation or that you excuse what has been done to you. Forgiveness is about releasing the anger so that you can open your heart for the future. Forgiveness is done mostly for you so that you no longer need to carry the burden of that pain. Similarly, you should ask for forgiveness from anyone you may have hurt. This, too, may be painful but will help you release yourself from any guilt you may be carrying around with you. Do your best to also settle all other financial debts and any other burdens you may have been carrying with you for so long. After all this you will be ready for some major celebration. Have a grand party in which you invite everyone you've ever known as a friend, partner, or acquaintance. Let it be a time when you revisit old memories. As a final bit of fun, be placed on a royal throne where others can tell stories about you, and then be crowned as the king or queen of the Jubilee.

Rituals for Life Cycles: The Crone/Sage

Name of ritual: Croning/Saging (Coming of Age III).

Best time: At around the 56th birthday, at the waning half moon.

General goals:

1. Honoring yourself and others.

Specific goals:

1. To reflect on what has been learned in life.

2. To consider how to pass wisdom on to others.

3. To determine a spiritual pilgrimage.

Possible blessings:

1. For continued health and wisdom.

2. To help others through passing on wisdom.

3. For a successful pilgrimage.

Items to use:

1. Gold working candle.

2. Four gifts in each of the elemental colors.

3. Large ritual circle.

4. Temporary tattoos.

5. A ritual gate.

6. Food for feasting.

7. The letter written at the second Coming of Age ritual.

Vows:

1. To act as an example of a wise Crone or Sage.

2. To pass on wisdom for the good of all beings.

Activities:

This is the third of three Coming of Age rituals that mark major milestones in the life of every person. Unlike the other two similar rituals, this ritual does not prepare or teach the celebrant anything. There is no need for that. There is only a recognition of the person as one who is full of experience and wisdom. To prepare for this ritual, the initiate should take time to review all past learning and wisdom. Create a large ritual working space. Have the initiate become temporarily tattooed with images that represent elderly life. Light your candle of intent. Have the initiate pass through the ritual gate and then go around the circle and receive praises from each of the four quarters. After each quarter, give the initiate a gift that represents that particular element. Others at the ceremony should be given a chance to also recognize the celebrant. At the end of the ceremony, the initiate should open the letter written at the second Coming of Age ritual. This may be read aloud or silently. A feast should follow the ceremony.

• • • • • • •

&> Name of ritual: Retirement.

Best time: When work retirement is accomplished.

General goals:

1. Honoring yourself and others.

Specific goals:

1. To review your accomplishments in work life.

Possible blessings:

    1. For an enjoyable retirement.

Items to use:

    1. Brown working candle.

    2. An item from work that you can burn.

Vows:

    1. To use the retirement time for spiritual pursuits and the chance to help others.

Activities:

This should probably be a ritual in two parts—one private and one public. The public part will be the typical retirement party, where your coworkers or friends wish you well for your retirement period. In a private ceremony, review those things that you did well through your work. Consider seriously how you can use the new addition of time to pursue your own goals and to help others. Find an item from work you can ritually burn to symbolize the end of the serious work life.

• • • • • • •

Name of ritual: Spirit Reckoning.

Best time: At around the 70th birthday, at the dark moon.

General goals:

    1. Honoring yourself and others.

Specific goals:

    1. To consider the meaning of death.

    2. To overcome the fear of death.

    3. To connect with past spirits.

Possible blessings:

1. For a peaceful passing.

2. For aid to those who will be left behind.

Items to use:

1. Black working candle.

2. Pictures of those who you have loved and who have passed on.

Vows:

1. To face death with courage.

2. To help others with the transition.

3. To live life fully to the end.

Activities:

If you have not already done so, make sure all physical preparations for your passing have been done. Light your candle of intent. Meditate on the meaning of death to you. It may help to read accounts of people who have almost died but returned to tell stories about the peacefulness of the death process. Connect with the spirits of those you have loved so that they can prepare your way. Resolve to overcome your fear of death so that you can live as fully as possible to its end.

Conclusion

In this book, you and I have taken a journey together to look into the very heart of Spirit and humanity. We have identified ways in which a complete and balanced Pagan spiritual practice can be created. Paganism has a very powerful and unique map of the way in which the universe works embedded in the circle of the equilateral cross and the four elements. With this map we have discovered different spiritual practices that can help to develop ourselves, each other, and the world in which we live. No spiritual practice can be complete if it does not include all these things. No matter how much anyone may practice his or her religion, an exclusive focus on self-development without a consideration for the wellness and wholeness of all beings creates only a hollow practice. All beings are connected—part of the same whole—and spiritual practice cannot separate this reality. Combining our Pagan way of life to all realms of relationships and all the cycles of life and living creates a beautifully intricate and connected practice. As we celebrate, honor, and worship these cycles, we become not just observers of them—we are fused with them. They become our life, and through them we observe the pulse of all life and the universe, we see the essence of Spirit through God and Goddess, and we dance with the divine.

Paganism is at an important threshold in history. What began as a curious look into ancient ways of worshipping nature has become a rapidly growing spiritual practice throughout the world. Ours may become a new world religion. With growth, however, comes growing pains. If we engage in too much bickering over the "right" way or the "correct" practice, we will be mired in our own confusion and become bogged down. A firm foundation is not created through single-mindedness (or narrow-mindedness), but in mutual respect, care, and support for each and for those who believe differently. If Pagans want to be respected, we must earn that respect by becoming living examples of truly caring and responsible spiritual people. Ours is a religion of love and respect for all beings, regardless of differences and divisions. Ours is a religion of tolerance. Ours is a religion that encourages diversity in thought and action. If we truly take to heart the dictum of "harm none," then ours is a religion of nonviolence: physically, mentally, emotionally, and spiritually. We must do more than talk about these things. We must live our values by honoring all life and its source. This is what is meant by living Paganism.

The world needs us. I firmly believe that the world needs what we Pagans offer. The world desperately needs people who care for Gaia and all Her children before both the planet and life are all wiped out by the belief that mankind is greater. The world badly needs to learn tolerance for all people, all religions, all colors, races, genders, creeds, sexualities, or whatever other means there are of separating ourselves. The world needs to once again honor these seasons and the changes in the moon. The world needs to return to a realization that all parts of the self are sacred—including the body—and that celebrating the wonders of the body is not bad. We need to live in a world where sin and guilt are replaced with reason and responsibility, religious intolerance is replaced by respect, meaninglessness in life is replaced by reverence and respect of all things, and existential dread is replaced by a joy for learning to be alive. This is what Paganism can offer the world, and it is what you can bring into your life.

Bibliography

Campanelli, Pauline. *Pagan Rites of Passage*. St. Paul, Minn.: Llewellyn Publications, 1998.

Eilers, Dana D. *The Practical Pagan*. Franklin Lakes, N.J.: New Page Books, 2002.

Heath, Robin. *Sun, Moon, & Earth.* New York: Walker and Company, 1999.

Higginbotham, Joyce and River. *Paganism: An Introduction to Earth-Centered Religions.* St. Paul, Minn.: Llewellyn Publications, 2002.

Johnson, Robert A. *Inner Work: Using Dreams and Creative Imagination for Personal Growth and Integration*. San Francisco: Harper, 1989.

Sessions, George. *Deep Ecology for the Twenty-First Century.* Boston: Shambhala, 1995.

Shanddaramon. *Self-Initiation for the Solitary Witch: Attaining Higher Spirituality Through A Five-Degree System.* Franklin Lakes, N.J.: New Page Books, 2004.

Thich Nhat Hanh. *Peace is Every Step: The Path of Mindfulness in Everyday Life.* New York: Bantam Books, 1991.

Walsh, Roger. *Essential Spirituality.* John Wiley and Sons, 1999.

Index

About the Author

SHANDDARAMON is a writer and artist living near Boston, Massa-
chusetts, where he teaches art, music, and Pagan studies classes. He also
teaches and does pastoral and divinatory advising and listening. He is a
founding member, brother, and ordained minister of the Sacred Order of
Living Paganism, a fellowship of brothers and sisters dedicated to deep
Pagan learning, practice, and service. He is a regular contributing writer
for PagaNet news.